The
SLIGHT

Praise from readers of *The Slight Edge*

As an instructor of a management course in a master's program at NYU, I made *The Slight Edge* required reading. It serves as the foundation for all other course content because I believe the philosophy is key to understanding success.
  —*David G Rosenthal, Advisory Board Member, Member Curriculum Committee; Adjunct Instructor; Chief Executive Officer, Shepard Communications Group, Inc.*

The Slight Edge is the book that makes every other personal-development book actually work. This is the REAL secret!
  —*Jesse Macpherson, Los Angeles, CA*

The Slight Edge was the single most formative influence on my career, health and happiness. I have gone back and read it over and over so many times that my copy is in complete tatters.
  —*Reed Herreid, Minneapolis, MN*

The Slight Edge freed me from the pressure I had put on myself for not maintaining the progress I made. For instance, all the years spent trying to lose weight and maintain. It was always a roller coaster, up and down, never any stability. But along came *The Slight Edge*. This put everything in perspective. I can go after anything and know that without a doubt I will be successful, because of *The Slight Edge*.
  —*Jimmy Williams, Austin, TX*

A unique view on how small changes or actions done repeatedly can change your personal, family and business life. An amazing and simple strategy anyone can apply, if they are willing.
  —*Pierre Rattini, North Myrtle Beach, SC*

I had read self-help books before and they did very little for me, so at first I didn't think this book would be much different. I was very wrong. This book has given me the power of wanting to have some failure in my life, and made me see the point behind the one penny. Before reading this book, I thought being average and unhealthy and overweight was just the life I was meant to live. I was very wrong. This book moved me in ways I never thought I could be. I wish I would have had it when I was 17.
  —*Tyra Snider, Canon City, CO*

It has created a sense of calm and peace for us, knowing we are on this Slight Edge journey to greatness. *The Slight Edge* has taught us the principle to be patient with ourselves, to look toward improving 1 percent at a time. It has taught us that positive and negative results don't happen overnight, but are cultivated through simple daily disciplines.
  —*Haas & Tahera Khaku, Anaheim Hills, CA, co-author, Power of Mentorship for the 21st Century*

The Slight Edge is the best personal-development book I have ever read.
  —*Michael Clouse, Seattle, WA*

This book is a treasure and I use it in every aspect of my life—business, personal, and fun!
  —*Shenna Shotwell, Creedmoor, NC*

The Slight Edge is a life philosophy that should be taught as soon as children take their first steps. I wish someone had taught me this when I was young.
  —*Jane Lehman, Lexington, MI*

I use this philosophy throughout my day. I've become a better person all around. I was able to correct my negative outlooks. I'm a better role model for my children, my health is getting better, I'm more connected spiritually, my relationships are improving, and my business is thriving. It is a must-have and a must-read.
—Pedro Garcia, Middletown, NY

I, like many people, get frustrated when I do not see quick results. Through the Slight Edge mentality, I was able to lose 25 pounds in just under three months. I also convinced my father, 69, who lost 20 pounds in less than three months. My father and I are both testimony to the fact that The Slight Edge works!
—Christopher Mangano, Boynton Beach, FL

I find the book to be one of the best "diet books" I have ever read, and I have read quite a few ot them through the last few years. So it is not willpower that is helping me to lose weight, it is The Slight Edge. What an amazing revelation this has been!
—Carol Chandler, Denver, CO

Before I read The Slight Edge, I never understood why my efforts seemed to be a degree off. The Slight Edge showed me how to get that last edge I needed!
—Lynda Cromar, Aurora, CO

The Slight Edge has had a profound effect on my life. After having it recommended four different times from four different people in one month, I finally purchased it. It was the first nonfiction book that I can remember not wanting to get to the end of because I loved what I was learning!
—Laura Jo Richins, Mesa, AZ

I was born and raised in Albania. I came to America 13 years ago at age 18 by myself, with nothing but a dream. I didn't speak English, and had no money or connections. I am a college dropout and a former pizza delivery driver. A friend gave me The Slight Edge book and by implementing its simple principles, I am today living the American Dream.
—Andi Duli, Oklahoma City, OK

The Slight Edge is truly a gift to the planet.
—Mark Skovron, Tampa Bay, FL

I was bankrupt, had my car repossessed, and was on Medicaid and applying for food stamps. After putting the principles of The Slight Edge in place, I have made over a million dollars and it has also helped me in every area of my life.
—Darin Kidd, Appomattox, VA

Reading The Slight Edge is perhaps one of the most eye-opening things one can do. It's such a simple concept that you realize you've overlooked every day of your life. Easy to do, easy not to do. Suddenly it's shocking how many things you really haven't been doing. The examples Jeff Olson provides are easy to understand and truly show how The Slight Edge affects the world.
—Julie Jonak, Houston, TX

I have read numerous personal-development books through the years, and by far, this is one of the best! By applying the principles of The Slight Edge, I've lost 35 pounds in just three months, and am still going strong. I'm also working them into my job, part-time pursuits and every area of my life. I have quit focusing as much on the goals, and am focusing more on the little things I do every day, since I can control those. As a result, my life is going SO much better than it ever has!
—Richard Green, Franklin, TN

This is a very simple, easy-to-follow book that can lead anyone from where they are to whatever level of success they want to achieve.
—*Alex Serrano, Las Vegas, NV*

Over the course of the last year, by putting the Slight Edge concepts in practice, I have stopped using tobacco, and lost 25 pounds through diet and exercise.
—*Bob Sutton, Ft. Collins, CO*

Following the principles outlined in Jeff Olson's *The Slight Edge* has helped me become a millionaire—several times over. Thanks for refining the processes into an understandable and workable format, Jeff.
—*Rex LeGalley, Albuquerque, NM*

The Slight Edge principles apply to everything.... My wife and I have used it to improve our health and now we have lost over 100 pounds combined!
—*BJ Baker, West Manchester, OH*

I led a life of errors in judgment until I came across this magnificent book. A blueprint for life can be founded on the Slight Edge philosophy. I found myself discarding old bad habits and replacing them with new positive habits; the result is a successful life. I was very reckless in my daily decisions, as well as my family positioning. My son noticed a huge change in my character and life perception. I no longer spend money haphazardly and my priorities are up to par.
—*Simon Ponce, Irvine, CA*

As a student of personal progress for the past 40 years, I consider this work to be one of the foundational keys to the application of literally every other resource in this incredibly important area of life.
—*Stephen McBroom, Floyd, VA*

The Slight Edge gives you that extra kick to push you beyond your wish list and into achieving your highest potential. I am able to apply the tools from *The Slight Edge* to balance my full-time work, while completing my bachelor's degree.
—*Mark Roberts, Redmond, WA*

The Slight Edge is a phenomenal book. It makes you aware of the unwritten rules that we all live by and just weren't aware of! A definite MUST READ for EVERYONE, from student to executive. Wondering why you can't pass a class? *The Slight Edge*! Tried those diets but just can't seem to lose the weight? *The Slight Edge*! Have a savings plan but your bank account just refuses to grow? *The Slight Edge*! When applied correctly, *The Slight Edge* will show you how to get things back on track in your life. You will now be aware of what you're doing and be armed with the knowledge to correct the important things in your life, from relationships to getting that executive promotion. The principles have definitely helped my life. Here's to your success!
—*Leonard Taylor, Las Vegas, NV*

Before reading *The Slight Edge*, my mindset for my life was not where it needed to be. I was a broke college student conforming to the masses. This book has changed the direction of my life dramatically by mentoring me on a new path filled with positive and disciplined philosophy.
—*Tim Walter, San Diego, CA*

After applying the Slight Edge, my life began to change for the better and I found myself harnessing the powers of completion and momentum every day. It was amazing to see results in my business, in my health, and in my personal life.
—*Carl Coffin, Goose Creek, SC*

I was searching for many answers to my life, when all of a sudden, I came across this magnificent and truthful information. It expanded my vision and took the fog away from my eyes.
    —*Michael Huerta, San Jacinto, CA*

As a successful leadership coach, I recommend two books to all of my clients. *The Slight Edge* is one of them!
    —*Dennis Antoine, Coral Springs, FL*

The Slight Edge kept me going on those days when I felt like I was not making progress by reassuring me that taking even the smallest positive action would eventually pay off.
    —*Susan Mix, Santa Clara, CA*

What an incredible masterpiece! *The Slight Edge* challenges me daily in business and in life. An absolute "must read" and "must apply" in every area.
    —*Dr. Vanessa R. Booker, Glendale, AZ*

The Slight Edge principles are so powerfully uplifting and inspirational that they are a catalyst for action. The Slight Edge gives me the momentum to achieve my daily goals in life.
    —*Antoinette Mims, New York, NY*

I have read personal-development books for over 20 years, and I can say this is the one that tied them all together, because it is so easy to read and understand, and so powerful in its simplicity.
    —*Mike Bishop, Wilsonville, OR*

The Slight Edge has been a philosophical staple in my life, and in the lives of those I mentor. I have started a business, and have gotten in better physical shape. The most memorable anecdote I use is, "What you do matters. What you do today matters. What do you every day matters."
    —*David Mack, Sacramento, CA*

I LOVE THIS BOOK! As a former professional athlete, coach for over 25 years and wellness consultant, I strongly recommend *The Slight Edge* to everyone. If you want success in your health, finances and relationships, embrace this book and create a new mindset, thereby a new future for yourself. *The Slight Edge* is empowering! The philosophies and thoughts will hit home with everyone who reads it.
    —*Lucy Del Sarto, Olathe, KS*

The Slight Edge is serving as a timeless way for me to help share the principles in which one must live to succeed in life. I have literally shared the concepts in this book with thousands.
    —*Ryan Chamberlin, Belleview, FL*

As a full-time police office I believe *The Slight Edge* mentality should be a part of the educational system across America.
    —*Bobby Garcia, Tucson, AZ*

This book has given me the vision to look past my current circumstances and into my desired results!
    —*Steven Joseph, St. Louis, MO*

The Slight Edge took years of personal-development study and rolled it all into one, easy to understand book. Jeff Olson did an awesome job of communicating how anyone in any profession can improve his/her productivity, personal relationships and family life. WOW!
    —*Brian Kennedy, Jacksonville, NC*

I would recommend *The Slight Edge* to anyone who is looking to understand why they have not been able to achieve their goals. They will understand that it is not all the fancy words many of the television hosts talk about, but the small things Mr. Olson writes about in his book—things that make absolute sense and are easy to do. I enjoy this book and have plans to make it part of my daily routine. I plan to give my family and myself a slight edge lifestyle. Thanks Mr. Olson.
    —*Glenn Watkins, Cibolo, TX*

I use the Slight Edge philosophy every day in my personal life and especially in my business. Doing the daily activities compounded over time has led me to the kind of success most people only dream about. As a single mother of three boys, it is the principles in this book that have made me over a million dollars in just a few short years, and have allowed me to achieve levels of success in business and in life. *The Slight Edge* will help anyone.
    —*Christa Aufdemberg, Orange County, CA*

The Slight Edge has given me and my family the secrets to a successful and abundant life. Practicing the basic philosophies of mastering the mundane has given my entire world a complete paradigm shift. There's a one-degree difference between hot and boiling, and this book has given me the necessary degrees to go from Good 2 Great. *The Slight Edge* is a lifer in my arsenal of personal development.
    —*Ken Hills, Syracuse, NY*

I found *The Slight Edge* to be a remarkable book. It was refreshingly different than other self-help books, as it focused on the hundreds of little daily and weekly decisions that build up to deliver the big hairy goals that one wants in life. My problem was that I can dream big and expect a lot from myself. But saying I wanted something huge next month and failing month after month just led to reluctance overall. Instead, after reading *The Slight Edge*, it was easier for me to focus on the daily schedule and on making daily progress.
    —*Timothy Sharpe, Redmond, WA*

I have used the principles of *The Slight Edge* to improve my physical fitness. I have used it to help pay off debt, build my savings and investments, and improve my relationships with my children.
    —*Stan Snow, North Yarmouth, ME*

I came across *The Slight Edge* and it instantly captured my attention. As an actress living in New York, it is so easy to get overwhelmed by everything that comes with this competitive business. *The Slight Edge* helped me to understand that the small choices I make every moment of every day make a huge impact on my life. Living in a society with so much emphasis on success, I found that *The Slight Edge* redefined what success is for me. It helps me to take the next step forward in my everyday life and do the next right thing. This ultimately leads to a very successful and fulfilling life. I attribute much of my success to the simple principles this book has outlined.
    —*Cara Cooley, Spokane, WA*

The SLIGHT EDGE

Turning Simple Disciplines
Into Massive Success

Jeff Olson

SUCCESS | BOOKS

This publication is designed to provide general information regarding the subject matter covered. However, laws and practices often vary from state to state and are subject to change. Because each factual situation is different, specific advice should be tailored to the particular circumstances. For this reason, the reader is advised to consult with his or her own advisor regarding their specific situation.

The author and publisher have taken reasonable precautions in the preparation of this book and believe the facts presented in the book are accurate as of the date it was written. However, neither the author nor the publisher assumes any responsibility for any errors or omissions. The author and publisher specifically disclaim any liability resulting from the use or application of the information contained in this book, and the information is not intended to serve as legal, financial or other professional advice related to individual situations.

Published by SUCCESS Books™, an imprint of SUCCESS Media.

SUCCESS | BOOKS

200 Swisher Road
Lake Dallas, Texas 75065
U.S.A.
Toll-free: 800.752.2030
Tel: 940.497.9700

The Slight Edge® is a registered trademark of The Meyer Resource Group, Inc. and is used under an exclusive license.

SUCCESS is a registered trademark and SUCCESS magazine and SUCCESS Books are trademarks of R&L Publishing, Ltd.

VideoPlus is a registered trademark of VideoPlus, L.P.

To order additional copies, visit www.SUCCESS.com.

Printed in the United States of America.

Book design by Amy McMurry

Library of Congress Control Number: 2005902199

ISBN: 978-1-935944-86-7

SPECIAL SALES
SUCCESS Books are available at special discounts for bulk purchase for sales promotions and premiums. Special editions, including personalized covers, excerpts of existing books, and corporate imprints, can be created in large quantities for special needs. For more information, contact Special Markets, SUCCESS Books, sales@success.com.

Contents

Acknowledgments

My thanks go to my mother, who has always believed in me; to Renée, my wife of eighteen years and now friend for life, who has always stood by me; and to our precious daughter Amber, who is our proudest accomplishment. They have all been my own personal Slight Edge.

A special thanks to Jim Rohn, whose teachings have had a profound impact on me. It's often his wisdom you hear in these words.

To John David Mann, my co-author, who brought his craft, passion, literary magic and good cheer to the project and made our book shine. To John Milton Fogg for his insights and his support, and for helping to get the ball rolling. To Todd Eliason and Reed Bilbray who brought their brilliance to this revised edition. To my close friend Stuart Johnson for helping this book, a dream of mine for many years, to finally come to pass.

To Amber Olson who has been the driving force in bringing to light this revised edition. It would not have happened without her passion and Slight Edge persistence. She continues to make me proud by living the Slight Edge in every area of her life.

And to all who know they have greatness deep inside them—and that it's just a Slight Edge away.

A special thanks to those already living the Slight Edge philosophy, many of whose stories you will read in this book. They are the inspiration for this revised edition and are living proof of the power of the Slight Edge.

Introduction:
The Missing Ingredient

The Shoeshine Woman

I arrived at the Phoenix airport about 6:30 in the morning. Having time before my plane left, I looked around to see if there was a place where I could get my shoes shined. There was hardly anybody in the airport at that time of the morning. I strolled around.

Before long, I found a shoeshine stand. It was open; a woman in her mid to late forties sat in one of the customer chairs, absorbed in a paperback book. She was dressed in black stretch pants, a black apron and a white shirt. She seemed like a nice, solid person.

I walked over to her stand.

The woman greeted me warmly. She was friendly and happy—*not always an easy way to be before the sun comes up*, I thought. She got up, set down her book, first carefully folding over the corner of the page she'd been reading, then took up the tools of her trade and pleasantly ushered me into the chair.

Her stand was located right next to a service door through which a constant stream of maintenance men and janitors came and went. *Got to be at work by seven*, I guessed. As they passed by our shoeshine stand, every one of these men stopped and exchanged greetings with the woman. She knew them all by name and they knew hers, too. It was clear they were all friends.

She went to work on my shoes, and we started talking.

Her daughter, she told me, had just won a cheerleading contest. Boy was she proud of her! The girl was hoping to go to a cheerleading camp in Dallas. "Tell you the truth," she confided, her voice dropping a bit, "I don't know how in the world I'm going to find the money to buy her the uniform and plane ticket, let alone the camp tuition."

In just the few minutes that I sat with this woman, I learned a good deal about her life—and about her. She loved her family, and for that matter, liked people in general. She made friends easily and was a natural-born communicator. It was also clear that she enjoyed her work.

And it's a good thing she does, I thought—because she'd been there, shining shoes in that same spot, for more than five years.

I couldn't help but wonder what this woman's life would be like if she had taken a different path five years earlier. She was well spoken, carried herself well, and was friendly and affable.

With different clothes and a little attention to her hair, she could easily pass for a successful businessperson.

I noticed the book she'd been reading. It was a popular novel, something to pass the time, to survive the stretches of occupational boredom by living vicariously in someone else's imagined romance. There was a little heap of them sitting dog-eared by the wall.

What if, instead of spending ten or fifteen minutes here and there, tucked in between customers, sinking into the pages of those forgettable novels, she had spent the last five years reading books that were genuinely life changing? What if that little stack of books included Napoleon Hill's Think and Grow Rich, *Stephen Covey's* The 7 Habits of Highly Effective People, *or David Bach's* Smart Women Finish Rich? *Where would she be today?*

The shoeshine woman was a hard worker. Good with people. She knew how to read and clearly enjoyed doing so. She was a superb communicator. She obviously had the talent, personality and basic life skills to accomplish a lot more than just living off tips from shining the shoes of people who could afford to buy their kids new uniforms and tickets to Dallas.

But she was spending her life building other people's dreams—not her own.

Your income tends to equal the average income of your five best friends, I mused. *What if she had spent time around people with significantly higher incomes than her own? What if, instead of hanging out only with her colleagues here in the airport, she had cultivated a different group of friends? What if she'd been associating with powerful people, successful people, mentors, movers, shakers, leaders? She could easily have done this—she's a terrific conversationalist. If she had, where would she be today?*

I'm not making a value judgment on modest incomes or simple occupations. There are people who work the humblest of jobs yet live lives rich in relationships and joy, just as there are extremely wealthy people who are also extremely unhappy. And I'm not criticizing popular novels. But it was clear that this woman was struggling, and as we sat there talking, I'd have bet anything that she wanted more out of life.

It was clear that she wanted to give her daughter the uniform and the Dallas trip, things she couldn't afford in the life she was living. And it was clear that it was so much on her mind, she'd confided her worries to a complete stranger within five minutes of meeting him.

She wanted more, it was plain to see. Why didn't she have it?

She's industrious, motivated and smart. She reads. She listens. She's sharp. Where would she be today if she'd set foot on a different path a year ago? Five years ago? You can bet she wouldn't be shining my shoes. Managing a chain of shoeshine stands is more like it. Would she be having any trouble sending her daughter to Dallas? I bet she'd be sponsoring the entire team—and going with them, too!

While this woman with the wonderful personality continued shining my shoes, I was watching her in my mind's eye, seeing her on a plane to Texas surrounded by giggling, excited, happy teenagers, seeing her being successful in so many different ways, in so many areas, making such a difference in her own life and the lives of so many others, if only ... what? What was missing?

Feelings welled up in me, a mix of frustration and sadness. I felt for a moment as if I were going to cry, and I wondered, *Why are you so moved by all of this? You've seen this before a hundred times—why are you so affected by this one instance?*

One reason, I knew, was that it reminded me of another character I'd observed before—nice, like the shoeshine woman, a good person ... just not succeeding in life.

The Beach Bum

I was born and raised in Albuquerque, New Mexico. My dad died when I was eleven; I remember being handed the flag from his casket. My mom held everything together; she was a great, loving mom. But it was still a rough way to grow up: a fatherless, blond-headed kid in a Hispanic neighborhood, who didn't fit in. I really didn't know what to do with it all, so I turned my energy into mischief and misbehavior: I blamed everything and everyone.

In third grade, my teachers informed my mom that I had a low IQ. I quickly gained a reputation for mischief and troublemaking. While my mom worked her way through the years, I struggled my way through school. By age eighteen, it was clear to anyone who knew me that I didn't have much of a future.

I begged my way into the University of New Mexico. At college, I built on my previous academic career and succeeded in taking my C average to a D average. I did learn one thing, though: I learned that when spring break came, all the students went to Daytona Beach for a week. I thought I could do one better—I quit school and moved there.

At Daytona Beach, I pursued my first profession: I became a beach bum. I lifted weights and chased girls. I let my hair grow long and curly. People started calling me "Gorgeous George," after the famous wrestler at the time.

I got a job at the Orlando Country Club cutting the grass on the golf course. One day, as I was cutting the greens in the hot Florida sun, I paused to watch the wealthy club members playing golf on the grass I had cut. As I watched them hum to and fro in their zippy golf carts, in dapper fine golf outfits, with their classy golf bags filled with expensive golf clubs, I felt a burning question simmer up inside.

Why is it that they're over there riding in carts, and I'm over here working? I don't get it. Why are they putting and I'm cutting? I don't get it! I'm as good as these people are. How do they get to have it ten times better than me? Are they ten times better than me? Are they ten times smarter? Or do they work ten times harder?

For whatever reason, as happens in so many people's lives, I found myself staring squarely at a fork in the road, a point I now refer to as a "day of disgust," that moment of impact we sometimes hit in our lives when we face our circumstances and make a decision to change.

In that instant, standing there sweating in the Florida heat, I came to a moment of decision. I suddenly knew that I'd had it up to here with where I was, what I was and who I was. Something clicked; the tumblers in the lock fell into place; and I knew that I could never go back to who I'd been only a minute earlier. I knew that for things to change, I had to change. For things to get better, I had to get better.

I left the golf course.

I loaded my stereo and clothes into my 1964 Dodge Dart slant-six (all my possessions fit easily into the back seat with room for a passenger) and took off for Albuquerque. It took me six days just to get to Texas because the car kept overheating. It was the longest trip of my life.

The Superachiever

That semester, for the first time in my life, I got straight A's. I went on to business school and graduated at the very top of my class. Fresh out of college, I became one of the youngest international airport managers in the country. I was then recruited by Texas Instruments (TI). I wanted to be in management, but they said, "If you want to be in management, you have to start in sales." Sales! I hated the idea of sales, knew nothing about it and was terrified of it, but sales it was.

I worked at TI for five years and went on to become Intelligent Systems Manager. But corporate America wasn't for me. There was a lot of politics (which I hated) and it did not feel like I'd yet found the place where I belonged.

I then decided to start a solar energy company. I knew nothing about solar energy; I barely knew whether the sun came up in the east or in the west. But with four hundred solar companies in the state, New Mexico was the capital of the budding new industry, so ignorance or not, the smart course of action seemed clear.

And at first, it looked like I had indeed made the smart decision. Within two years, my company was in the top 20, and eventually we became the fifth-largest solar-air energy company in America. I was thrilled. I was on top of the world. What I did not yet know was that nothing ever stays the same: everything is in motion. Everything changes.

Times changed. Tax laws changed. Our industry was hit hard. Before I knew what was happening, I had lost everything, gone back to zero and below—owing more money than I thought I could ever even hope to make again.

The Lesson

The night my car was towed away, I sat in despair and thought:

This just isn't fair. After living as a failure all my life, I woke up one day and came to my senses, went back to college, applied myself like crazy, entered at the bottom and graduated at the top, worked for a major corporation for five years and went to the very top, built my own company in less than five years and went to the top … and here I am, after twelve long years of building toward success, at the bottom again! I'm more broke today than when I was Gorgeous George on the beach!

Twelve years of blood and guts, and I was more of a failure than ever. I couldn't wrap my head around it. I couldn't see the logic, the justice, the reasons for any of it. Was life just inherently unfair? Was that it? Was there simply no rhyme or reason for anything? Was there no point in even trying?

That was when I began to examine more carefully what had happened in my life.

I had been a college dropout, a beach bum and a complete financial failure. And I had also been a straight-A student, a top corporate manager, a super-achieving entrepreneur in a cutting-edge industry and a complete financial success. And all of those had been the same person. So what was the difference? It made no sense.

Or did it?

For the first time, I began to see that over the years of my roller-coaster career, I had gone through a rich sequence of experiences that held the secrets to success as well as to failure. I had proven to myself, beyond any shadow of doubt, the depths of failure that simple daily errors in judgment could produce. I had also seen what simple daily disciplines could accomplish. I just hadn't quite realized what I knew.

It was time to pull away the veil of circumstance and look right at the heart of the matter. To go behind the results and examine the actions, and behind the actions to find the attitudes, and behind the attitudes to discover the thinking that held them there.

That was when I began to discover and explore the Slight Edge.

Since that time, I have built some extraordinary businesses and earned more money than I ever dreamed of back when I was a corporate manager or solar energy entrepreneur. I've also experienced more joy and fulfillment within my family and other relationships than I knew was possible. I've also discovered new vistas in my own investment in my own development, in terms of both health and learning.

Perhaps most important of all is that I've built a philosophy that is grounded in reality, in the way things actually work—not on luck but on the power of the simple disciplines.

I could lose it all tomorrow. (It's happened before; I'd survive.) But there is something I cannot lose, and with that one thing I could start from scratch and build it all back up again. That one thing is the Slight Edge.

If Only ...

"You're lookin' good, sir, lookin' good."

The shoeshine woman was grinning at me. *Another customer lost in his early morning thoughts. And another job well done.* I looked down: I could see my reflection in my shoes.

Indeed I am. Lookin' good ... thank you. Thanks very much.

I paid her, gave her as big a tip as I could without (I hoped) having her feel I was being patronizing, and walked away with clean shoes and a heavy heart.

She was right; for me, things were lookin' good, sir, lookin' good.

But why the beach bum and not the shoeshine woman?

While my shoes had been getting a shine, the airport had grown busier. I now walked through a growing throng of travelers as I worked my way toward my gate. I noticed all the faces filing past me. Hardly anyone was smiling. Most of my fellow travelers were trudging with their heads bowed down. I saw bored expressions. Vacant. *Porch light's on, dog's barking, but nobody's home.*

Everybody looked so tired. Failing is exhausting.

I heard angry words.

I stopped for a cup of coffee and heard a young couple arguing with each other. A burly man scolded his young son to the point of tears. A heavy woman complained about the service, then the prices, then her food, and then started back in on the service again. The other people in line nodded their heads. A few joined her in a chorus of negativity.

Why is everyone so ... down? Everything these people need to know to change their lives for the better is already available. All the information they could possibly need to put them on a path of extraordinary success and fulfillment is out there, in books and CDs, DVDs and workshops. There are people to help them—rich, living resources to guide them, be their mentors, teachers, coaches and allies.

I knew that the difference between who they were and who they could be wasn't based on any lack of good information. It was all already available.

But why, if the information is all there, all the resources are there, and these people really do want to succeed, aren't they doing it?

I looked around the airport as the early morning rush hour swelled its ranks of busy, hurrying, scowling, unhappy people shambling past with no spark in their faces, no bounce in their step. I wished I could somehow address them all, that I could touch all their lives with my silent soliloquy.

The problem, I shouted out in my head, *is that you don't have a way to process the information. There's no framework in place for you to take in all the extraordinary insight that's out there and put it to work in your life.*

If only you were aware of the Slight Edge. If only you knew what it was doing in your life and how easy it is to have the Slight Edge working for you—instead of against you.

If only you were making the right choices, doing those simple, little disciplines that would change your life for the better forever ... where would you be five years from today?

If only you learned to recognize the Slight Edge ...

If only ...

But it was only in my head. Not a soul heard my words ... nobody, that is, but me.

That day, on the plane, I started writing this book.

The Slight Edge is not just more good information. It's not another self-help success book packed with some revolutionary "new best way" of doing things. You don't need that. Nobody needs that. All the "new and better" information is already available and has been for years.

This book is a precursor to help you use that information.

This book is what I hope will help you take whatever information you want, whatever how-to's or strategies or goals or aspirations, and turn them into the life you want. This book is what I wish I could have put into that sweet and sad shoeshine woman's hands.

I have since been back to that airport. In fact, I have been back through there many, many times. I have looked for the shoeshine woman, but she is no longer there. I don't know where she is or what has happened in her life. But I do know this: she is not alone. There are millions upon millions of people, everywhere I go, everywhere I look, whose lives are not all that they wish, not all that they yearn for. Not even close.

And yet they could be.

So I dedicate this book to that shoeshine woman, to her daughter, to her daughter's cheerleading team ... and to everyone else in the world who wants more.

I dedicate this book to *you and to those who have already put the Slight Edge into practice.*

Foreword:
The Road to the Slight Edge

It's been some time now since my encounter with the shoeshine lady, and a lot has happened since then. I have been fortunate to be the CEO and owner of many successful companies. So how did I get there? Well, I've had some help. When you get the opportunity to be around successful CEOs and influential authors and speakers, their wisdom has a way of rubbing off on you.

But the main reason for my success—and the success of other influential people around the world—continues to be the daily application of the philosophy I am going to share with you called the Slight Edge.

After my time at Texas Instruments and building my own company Sun Aire of America, which at the time was one of the largest solar energy companies in the country, I went on to build three separate multimillion-dollar sales forces, one of which I was appointed CEO.

Based on that experience, I founded TPN (The People's Network), which was one of the largest personal-development training companies in the nation, producing over 900 television programs on various topics such as family relationships and finance, etc. As the CEO of TPN I was often regarded as one of the most influential people in personal development. I eventually sold TPN to a New York Stock Exchange company.

I then took the principles I learned at TPN to help consult for a company, and I have been instrumental in taking them from $70 million in revenues to $500 million.

I arrived at these destinations, not by being smarter than everyone else, not by quantum leaps of advancement, but by consistently applying the Slight Edge philosophy.

The Pinnacle of Personal Development

As CEO and founder of TPN I had the opportunity to meet with many of the greatest masterminds and thinkers of our time. Influential authors and speakers were lining up at my door, due to the large distribution of personal-development information our company produced. I sat with Oprah Winfrey for lengthy in-depth discussions on the path of personal development. I spent a weekend with Dick Snyder, then CEO of Simon & Schuster (the largest publisher of personal development), in his mansion in the woods of Connecticut, discussing everything there is to discuss about personal development. I worked closely with Jan Miller, the biggest literary agent of personal development. I even went to Nashville, the capital of country music, to talk with legendary country music executive Jimmy Bowen about mixing personal development with music.

I met with about every leading author and speaker on every topic you can imagine, many of whom made appearances in many of our programs. TPN was making huge waves. I was on the cover of *The Wall Street Journal* as well as many other publications, including *Entrepreneur* magazine and *SUCCESS* magazine, discussing what TPN was accomplishing in the personal-development world.

Does *Chicken Soup for the Soul* sound familiar? It should; this one book has sold over 100 million copies and has spawned several other titles that have been translated into several languages. I was there in 1993 when author Mark Victor Hansen shared with me his idea and dream to create the *Chicken Soup for the Soul* series.

I don't bring up these examples just to brag or to drop names; I do it to explain what all these experiences have afforded me: a rare opportunity to absorb and amass information from the very best on every topic imaginable, and see it all from the catbird seat. We were not just information providers but information producers. What I came to realize is that information about how to become successful has always been readily available, but if the person absorbing that information doesn't have the right philosophy to apply it the right way, success will elude their grasp.

You see, there is no magic bullet, quick fix, or quantum leap method to reach success. Marketing tactics are used to pull us in to "lose 30 pounds in 3 weeks" or "make money while you sleep." The only problem? Although some might have success in the beginning, the results are not long lasting, This ends up frustrating the consumer and makes them give up on otherwise great information, that if applied with the right philosophy would have given them great results.

What the Slight Edge philosophy is meant to do is give you a philosophy that will become a filter for every decision you make. It will give you a way to apply great information into your life in a way that will produce lasting results. It is the missing ingredient to making change happen! If you understand the Slight Edge philosophy then you can effectively apply any sound principle or action into your life with success. And that is a 100 percent guarantee. In fact, if after putting the principles to work in your own life you don't see improvement, we will refund every penny you paid for this book.

I have been teaching the Slight Edge philosophy for many years now, and published the first edition of the book in 2005. Many great things have been birthed from *The Slight Edge*: The SUCCESS Foundation (www.successfoundation.org) was created to provide teens with the fundamental principles of personal development and the resources to help them reach their full potential.

The organization even wrote the book *SUCCESS for Teens: Real Teens Talk About Living The Slight Edge*, and have teamed up with stellar organizations such as Big Brothers Big Sisters, Boys & Girls Clubs, Network for Teaching Entrepreneurship, Just Say Yes, America's Promise Alliance and Optimist International to get *The Slight Edge* principles into the hands of millions of teenagers.

Two of the people I mentored at TPN, Darren Hardy and Kym Yancey, and many others have gone on to do some great things. Darren went on to become the publisher of *SUCCESS* magazine and authored a book *The Compound Effect* based on the Slight Edge philosophy. Kym, along with his wife Sandra, created E-Women Network, recognized as the No. 1 resource for connecting and promoting women and their businesses worldwide. Another good friend, Todd Smith, penned a great book called *Little Things Matter*, based on the Slight Edge principles. These are wonderful books and I encourage you to go buy them to learn more about their interpretation of the Slight Edge philosophy.

Many other readers of *The Slight Edge* have gone on to accomplish amazing things by simply implementing the Slight Edge principles in their lives—many of the stories we will share with you in this revised edition.

Origin of *The Slight Edge*

Over the years many people have asked me how *The Slight Edge* was conceived. It began when the book was only a concept. To flesh it out I went to the Mountain Shadow Resort in Phoenix to get away by myself and spent a weekend listening to Jim Rohn and other legendary personal-development icons. Soon I started to see an overall philosophy develop from all that I read and heard that weekend. I didn't have a name for it, and I couldn't write down in words what it meant at the time. The best way to convey it was to simply draw it out.

Slight Edge Life Paths

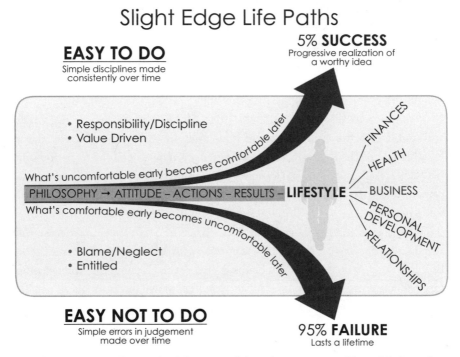

EASY TO DO
Simple disciplines made
consistently over time

5% **SUCCESS**
Progressive realization of
a worthy idea

- Responsibility/Discipline
- Value Driven

What's uncomfortable early becomes comfortable later

PHILOSOPHY → ATTITUDE – ACTIONS – RESULTS – **LIFESTYLE**

What's comfortable early becomes uncomfortable later

- Blame/Neglect
- Entitled

FINANCES
HEALTH
BUSINESS
PERSONAL DEVELOPMENT
RELATIONSHIPS

EASY NOT TO DO
Simple errors in judgement
made over time

95% **FAILURE**
Lasts a lifetime

Once on paper I came back home and drew it out on my office whiteboard to further flesh out the concept. From this crude drawing I started to teach it out on the road and it soon became known as the Slight Edge.

Everywhere I went people wanted me to give the Slight Edge speech. My next task was to get it out of my head and onto paper so people could read it whenever they wanted. I wrote the first 120 pages and then life got busy and the unfinished manuscript sat on my credenza for years. Eventually I carved out the time to finish it.

What I'm about to say next is going to surprise you. I was never trying to create a best seller with *The Slight Edge*. I was simply trying to get it out of my brain and onto paper as fast as I could so people would stop hounding me about it. This way I could point to the book without having to explain the entire philosophy.

First, I sent the book out to a few friends who wanted it, thinking that would be it. But I received more calls from my friends telling me how much they got out of reading the book, which I laughed at. I discounted much of what they were saying because these were my close friends and I figured they were just being supportive.

But then I started getting calls from people who had received the book from my close friends, and it mushroomed from there. All this time others were telling me this, but I was too busy to notice. That's when it hit me that we were on to something. However, my daughter would say the day she knew we were on to something was when she saw *The Slight Edge* listed on ABC's website as *The Bachelorette* contestant

Roberto Martinez's favorite book. When he went on to win the show and Ali's heart she called me and said "The Slight Edge even helps you win reality TV shows!"

In all seriousness, the amazing thing is we hardly promoted the book. In fact, it never had wide distribution because it could only be purchased by calling a 1-800 number. By simple word-of-mouth the book has exploded at a grassroots level— completely organic. And now that we have seen how it is affecting so many lives I wanted to make it better—to take it to the next level.

And if wasn't for my daughter Amber pushing me to bring some of these stories and testimonials to life, this revised edition wouldn't exist. She was the driving force behind this project and pushed me to make this book even better than it already is.

The Book That Started It All

The message I want to get across is this book is real. Over the years, people have shared with me how the Slight Edge was working in their life. I told them to give me their business card with the topic (either finances, health, sports, etc) on the back and we would call them to get their story in writing. Let's just say I didn't do a very good job in calling these wonderful people back. Amber finally volunteered to call these people when she saw the drawer spilling over with business cards of people anxious to share their stories.

Again, I want to thank my daughter for finding the time to call these wonderful people and to personally thank them for sharing with me the stories you are about to read.

I would be remiss if I didn't give credit to the time period when *The Slight Edge* debuted. Personal-development sections of bookstores exploded in the '90s and we were a part of that exciting time. People had finally begun to ask themselves, *What I am doing with my life? I want something more.* Today we are experiencing a similar revival. In time of economic distress, people start to prioritize what's most important to them and they want to be educated on how to get ahead.

I tell you all this so that before I start explaining the Slight Edge philosophy you get to see how I came to understand the Slight Edge and how these principles have stood the test of time by themselves—with or without my influence—and have enabled people to accomplish amazing things. The principles you are about to learn are time-tested, and it's my deepest desire that you will embrace them to the fullest.

As a way to thank all of the readers, this revision is dedicated to all the past, present and future readers of *The Slight Edge*. All we have done is plant the seed. You are the ones who have watered and cultivated it to be what it is today.

Thank you,
Jeff Olson

What's New in This Revised Edition?

In this revised edition we have meticulously gone through each chapter and expanded it with new stories, as well as updates based upon observation of the Slight Edge principles over the last five years.

There is a new chapter in this edition called 7 Slight Edge Principles. It's a collection of specific, actionable principles and characteristics that will help you in applying the Slight Edge philosophy, which Part Two of the book is all about. It is a good foundation on which to start your own personal-development journey, all the while creating a positive ripple effect, by one action that creates several positive reactions.

The one thing I am most excited about in this revised edition is the chance to share with you the stories of many readers of *The Slight Edge*. We have received thousands of amazing stories from readers explaining how *The Slight Edge* has helped them with their personal relationships, finances, business, health, and life pursuits just by injecting the Slight Edge philosophy into their lives. The results have created a ripple effect having a lasting impact on everyone they meet. Their stories explain the principles and real-life applications far better than I ever could. I hope you will be moved by their stories as much as I was.

My daughter Amber contributed a section addressing the next generation of readers of *The Slight Edge*. She has grown up with *The Slight Edge* and knows the importance of getting this information into the hands of young people to help them understand that the choices they make today will affect the rest of their lives.

> *Through my father and others, I have seen the impact of a lifetime full of right and wrong decisions and where they lead you. I am forever grateful to have had the Slight Edge philosophy instilled in me at a young age by my parents, because I was able to end up on the positive side of the Slight Edge curve by being aware that the choices I make on a daily basis matter.*
>
> —Amber Olson

I am excited and honored to announce the brand new Slight Edge online community, an additional resource that gives readers of *The Slight Edge* a voice to share their experiences with other like-minded individuals, as well as share resources and Slight Edge tips, encourage and support one another, and experience additional life-enriching information. **Please come experience the slight edge community at www.SlightEdge.org**. I look forward to seeing you there!

Three Stories

The Water Hyacinth

The water hyacinth is a beautiful, delicate-looking little plant. Prized as an ornament, it sports six-petaled flowers ranging from a lovely purplish blue, to lavender, to pink. You can find it floating on the surface of ponds in warm climates around the world.

The water hyacinth is also one of the most productive plants on earth; its reproductive rate astonishes botanists and ecologists. Although a single plant can produce as many as 5,000 seeds, the method it prefers for colonizing a new area is to grow by doubling itself, sending out short runner stems that become "daughter plants."

If a pond's surface is fairly still and undisturbed, the water hyacinth may cover the entire pond in thirty days.

On the first day, you won't even notice it. In fact, for the first few weeks you will have to search very hard to find it. On day 15, it will cover perhaps a single square foot of the pond's surface ... a barely significant dollop of color dotting the expanse of placid green.

On the twentieth day (two-thirds of the way to the end of the month), you may happen to notice a dense little patch of floating foliage, about the size of a small mattress. You would be easily forgiven if you mistook it for a boy's inflatable life raft, left behind during a family picnic.

On day 29, one-half of the pond's surface will be open water.

On the thirtieth day, the entire pond will be covered by a blanket of water hyacinth.

You will not see any water at all.

Two Frogs

One night, two frogs left the safety of their swamp and ventured into a nearby farm to explore. They soon found themselves in a dairy. Hopping and jumping around (frogs will be frogs, after all), they jumped into a milk pail half full of cream.

At first, they were both thrilled. They had never tasted anything so delicious! They drank and drank. Soon (after some contented frog belches followed by much giggling) they were both full-bellied and getting just a bit sleepy. "Time to get out of here and head back to the swamp for some shut-eye," burped the first frog.

But there was a problem. They'd had no trouble hopping in ... but how to hop out? The inside of the pail was too slippery to climb, and there was nothing on which they could place their feet for traction to get up a good hopping distance ... or any hopping distance at all.

The awful reality dawned on them: they were trapped.

Frantic, they began to thrash about, their little frog feet scrabbling for a foothold on the elusive, slippery curve of the pail's edge.

Finally, the second frog cried out, "It's no use! We're doomed, my brother! Let us save what dignity we have left and die here like frogs, with our eyes facing our homeland!"

The first frog cried out to stop him. "No! We should never give up! When we were tadpoles, which of us would ever have dreamed that some day we would emerge from the water and hop about on land? Swim on, and pray for a miracle!"

The second frog eyed his brother sadly and said, "There are no miracles in the life of a frog, brother. Farewell." And so saying, he turned his face in the direction of the swamp, gave a sigh, and slowly sank out of sight.

But the first frog refused to give up.

He continued to swim. He swam and he swam in ridiculous, pointless, useless, futile circles, hoping against hope for a miracle. Fired by adrenaline, he paddled mightily ... yet his brother's dying words clutched at his thoughts, even more insidious than the growing fatigue that tugged at his weakening muscles. *Was my brother right?*, he thought desperately. *Am I a fool? Are there no miracles in the life of a frog?*

Finally, he could swim no more ... and with a great cry of anguish, he stopped paddling and let go, ready at last to face his fate like a frog.

But something odd then happened ... or rather, *didn't* happen. He didn't sink. He just sat exactly where he was. Ever so tentatively, he stretched out a foot ... and felt it touch something solid.

He heaved a big sigh, both sad and grateful, said a silent farewell to his drowned brother, then scrambled up on top of the big lump of butter he had just finished churning ...

... and hopped out of the pail and off to the swamp, alone but alive.

The Choice

A wealthy man nearing the end of his days summoned his twin sons to his bedside. Before he died, he told them, he wanted to pass on to them the opportunity to experience the richness of life that he had enjoyed for his many years on earth.

"If I could do so, I would give you both the world," he told his boys, "but this is not possible, for even I do not own the entire world and everything in it. But there are three treasures I have had the good fortune to experience in my life, and it is my fondest wish, my dying wish, that you would both have these three treasures.

"The first gift is easy to give, and never runs out. I have been giving it to you both since you were born, and die in peace knowing that you both already have it in abundance.

"The second gift is easy to give, but not always easy to have. For some, it never runs out, while for others, it constantly runs out. This gift I give you now, but whether or not you keep it will be up to you.

"The third gift is impossible to give, but can only be gained. I have been showing it to you both your entire lives, but cannot say whether or not you have gained it. This gift I cannot give you, but I can give you an opportunity to see it one last time before I die."

The boys both wept to hear their father speak of his approaching death, but he smiled and bade them hush with a wave of his hand.

"I see your grief, but in that grief you may be happy, for it is evidence of the first gift, which you have in abundance. Do you know what the first gift is?"

The two boys dried their tears and furrowed their brows in deep thought. *Easy to give, and it never runs out ...*

Suddenly the first boy clapped his hands and said, "Love! The first gift is love!" The father smiled. The boy was right. "And the second gift?" he asked them.

They again became quiet with thought. *Easy to give, but not always easy to have ...*

The second boy looked up with a start. "Money? Is the second gift money?" It was indeed. *For some, it never runs out, while for others, it constantly runs out.*

"And the third?"

Impossible to give, can only be gained ...

This time both boys remained buried in thought. Neither could come up with an answer.

The father smiled again, a little sadly this time. He lifted a beautiful lacquer box from the bedside table onto his lap, opened it and looked inside.

"I offer you both a choice."

He beckoned the boys to move closer.

"One month from today, you both will turn twenty-one. I will no longer be with you, for my life has run its course. On that day, thirty-one days from now, I have instructed my most trusted advisor to execute a document that will bequeath my home, my treasury, my estate—all that I possess—to the good people of this land, who have treated me with kindness all these years. This place, which has been our home together for these twenty-one years, will become a public trust. I will be well on my way to the next world, and the two of you will set off to make your way in this one.

"Yet I do not wish you to set foot on this journey empty-handed. My last gift to you, on the day of your departure, will be a purse to finance your adventures.

"What goes into each purse is your choice."

He reached both hands inside the box, and then held them out to the boys. In one hand, he held a sheaf of one thousand crisp, new $1,000 bills. One million dollars. Cash. In the other hand, he held a shiny new copper penny.

"If you take the million in cash, you may take it with you or leave it in your purse for safe-keeping until the day of your journey; your purse will be held by my treasury director.

"If you take the penny, you may also take it with you or leave it in your purse. However, if you choose the penny, my treasury director has instructions to double the contents of your purse every day."

He took out another lacquer box, identical to the first, opened it, and took out another stack of $1,000 bills and another penny.

"Here is one million; here is one penny. You each have the same choice to make. Whatever you do not take, I will return to my treasury to add to my estate.

"Now, go, rest, and think. Tomorrow morning, come back and tell me your choice."

All night, the first boy lay in bed thinking, *What should I do? Which should I take? What is the lesson?* The second boy lay awake, too, but he asked himself different questions. He had made his decision before his father had finished the sentence. Now he was making careful plans for what to do for the next thirty-one days.

When morning came, the second boy sprang into action. After securing the million in cash from his father, he hired a sharp consultant and a manager to help him execute his carefully wrought plan. They rented out a hotel suite, in which they conducted exhaustive, back-to-back interviews for the next six days. By week's end, they had hired a staff of the finest financial advisors in the land.

The boy's new crackerjack money-man team spent the second week in intensive, round-the-clock brainstorming sessions, drafting proposal after proposal, seeking the smartest, most cost-effective investment and leveraging strategies, both long-term and short-term, to help the wealthy man's son turn his million into a genuine fortune.

By week three, the best plans had been selected, winnowed, examined, combed, explored, game-theoried, road-tested, computer-simulated and dissected. With all their i's dotted and all their t's crossed, the boy's advisors were locked and loaded and ready to rumble. Off they went, into the battlefields of commerce and speculation. The boy spent the next few days keeping in close contact with his far-flung financial team by telephone; but by mid-week, it seemed clear that things were well in hand and he was not needed. He decided to pay a visit to his brother, whom he had not seen since breakfast on the morning after that long and sleepless night.

When he arrived at their home, he was shocked to hear his brother's account of the past few weeks.

After that excited breakfast, the first boy had also paid a visit to his father, but without explaining why, he announced that he had made the second choice. He had taken the penny, left it in the purse, then returned to his room and began reading from one of his favorite books.

The second day, he visited again, and was allowed to peek into the purse: the shiny new penny had been joined by a companion. On the third day, he found four pennies. On the fourth, there were eight, and on the fifth, sixteen, then thirty-two.

By the end of the week, just as his brother's ace financial team was assembling in the beautiful hotel suite for the first time, he had amassed a nest egg of sixty-four cents. By the end of week two—with nearly half the month gone—his piles of pennies had swelled to just shy of ninety dollars ... $81.92, to be exact.

On the day his brother's financial team hit the streets and went out into the world ready to turn his million into billions, his purse had not yet accumulated a hundred dollars—he would not have been able to purchase even a decent dinner for two at the fine hotel where his brother's suite had been humming with action for two weeks.

Now, a few days into the third week, the purse's contents had grown a bit more: he now had a sum of $655 ("and thirty-six cents," he proudly pointed out)—easily enough to sustain him on the road for a full week.

"But you poor sap!" his brother cried on hearing his story. "I can't believe you went for the penny! It's not too late—visit our father, see if he will relent and give you your own million. Or if he insists in prorating the amount, then even just half the million—it's better than scrabbling by on a few paltry hundred! And if he refuses, you've got to let me help ... I can't stand the idea of you venturing out into the world with scarcely enough to feed yourself for a week!"

But the brother seemed unperturbed and wouldn't hear of it.

Later that week, the wealthy man called his sons to him one more time and spent several hours with them, sharing memories and telling stories. They both left him in good spirits (though the second boy was secretly very worried about his brother's prospects).

That night, the old man died peacefully in his sleep.

Toward the end of week four, the second boy's top advisors brought him some worrisome news. The markets, it seemed, had gone a bit soft. Taken a bit of a tumble, actually. The team had acted quickly and salvaged what they could, but their earlier rosy projections would most certainly need to be revised downward.

The boy thanked them for their vigilance, and waited, fretting and anxious.

At the close of the week, the team brought mixed news. Some investments had performed quite well, others had suffered. All in all, the boy had made a modest gain: starting with his one million in cash, his team had succeeded in parleying that into nearly one and a half million. Unfortunately, his expenses, including their commissions, tax, bills for the hotel suite, broker fees and the rest, came to just over half a million.

The boy had ended the month with just a bit less than he started!

In a panic, he rushed to see his brother, to see how he had fared with his $655 (and thirty-six cents)—only to receive yet another shock. On day 28, his brother's purse of pennies had passed the million-dollar mark. On day 29, the two-and-a-half million mark. Yesterday, on day 30, it had doubled to *more than five million!*

The boy who chose the penny had discovered the extraordinary power that some have called "the eighth wonder of the world"—the remarkable creative force of *compound interest.*

And today, the boy who chose the penny was worth more than *ten* million dollars—$10,737,418 ... and twenty-four cents.

A Question

Two boys. Two frogs. Two powerful choices. Riches or poverty. Life or death.

You are making those same choices, every day, every hour, and the choices you make are spreading out through your life, just like the water hyacinth. You may not see the results today, or tomorrow, or even next year. In fact, by the time you do finally see the results, the process will probably be so far along that the surface of the pond will be completely covered.

The question is, covered with what?

When the wealthy man spoke to his sons, the second boy thought he was offering them a choice of *which money* to take. But the first boy listened more carefully. He remembered that money was only the second gift. He understood that the choice was not whether to take the penny or the sheaf of bills—the choice was whether or not to take the third gift.

Wisdom.

The lesson was not about money: it was about wisdom. It was a lesson about compound interest, leverage, geometric progression and growth. It was a lesson about the Slight Edge.

The choice the wealthy man offered his two sons is the same choice the world offers you, every day, every hour: sickness or health; sinking poverty or abundant wealth; deepening loneliness and alienation or a rich and growing circle of friends.

The Slight Edge will be your guide to the wealthy man's third gift; it will help you learn habits of thought and action that will allow you to choose the penny doubled, every time. It will keep you paddling until your cream becomes butter. It will give you the power to choose what to plant in your life, so that you will end up completely blanketing the surface of the pond with the blossoms of your choice.

PART ONE

The Slight Edge

CHAPTER 1

The Slight Edge Philosophy

The law of nature is, Do the thing, and you shall have the power: but they who do not the thing have not the power.

—Ralph Waldo Emerson, *Compensation* (Essays: First Series, 1841)

Take two seemingly similar people and give them both the exact same opportunity. One takes it and has remarkable success, the other doesn't. One wins, the other does not.

Why?

During my years in business, I've worked with several thousand people from every imaginable walk of life. They have all had the exact same opportunity. (A number of these people have become millionaires, to the point that somewhere along the way I picked up the nickname "The Millionaire Maker.") Many more people I have worked with have earned a good, solid living. But the great majority of them, faced with exactly the same opportunities, have gone nowhere.

Why? It's not a matter of luck. Nor is it timing, nor fate. It's not a matter of intelligence, skill or talent, either.

During these same years, I've risen to the very top with many different companies, with different product lines, in different countries and different languages (which I don't speak). In case you're worried that I'm bragging, let me put your mind at ease: there was absolutely nothing brilliant about what I did. Actually, it was quite the opposite. In every case, I did the exact same thing every time, using ridiculously simple strategies made up of ridiculously simple lists of ridiculously simple actions.

And in case you're now thinking that I'm exaggerating, that those are statements of false modesty, let me put your mind at ease about that, too. The strategies I used—none of them invented or devised by me, incidentally—are so simple that if you and I sat down together in a room for twenty minutes, I could show you exactly what I did to create four different, separate, independent multimillion-dollar organizations—and teach you how to do the exact same thing. In twenty minutes.

And chances are, it wouldn't work for you.

Why not? Because how to do it is not the issue. Because, if we don't change the way you think, then you'll have rearranged what I said by the time you leave the room. You'll have reinvented it by the time you go to bed that night and in the morning, you won't even recognize it as the same information.

People everywhere are clamoring for the formula, the secret, the path to improve their lives. *Tell me how you did this, so I can do it, too. Give me the definitive plan. Tell me how to be healthy. Tell me how to be rich. Tell me how to be happy. Tell me, tell me, tell me* ... and there's more good, solid how-to information available today about all those things than there's ever been in history. But that's not how it works. If you're one of the millions looking for cookie-cutter answers to the great questions in life, you can call off the search right now! *How to do it* is not the issue.

If "how to do it" were the answer, it'd be done. **It's how you do the "hows" that's most important.** If access to the right information were the answer, we'd all be rich, healthy, happy and fulfilled. And most of us are none of those things.

Why not? Because the answer is only the answer—it isn't actually doing the thing. It isn't *applying* the answer, *living* the answer. It's only information.

It's not that how-to books are not valuable; there are some wonderful ones I'll even recommend to you at the end of this book. It's just that another how-to book is not what you need. It's not what any of us need. We already have enough of those—maybe more than enough. Because what you need to transform your life is not more information.

Besides, we're all so different; my how-to may not be yours. It may work for me, but it may not be the how-to that works for you. As much as we'd all love to quantify a precise, specific, paint-by-the-numbers approach to life, love and happiness, we are out of luck in that department because there is no universal, one-size-fits-all method to anything. However ...

The Secret Ingredient

However, there is a secret ingredient.

There is a secret that, once you know it, will cause you to find those answers, apply them, live them, and achieve those results you want.

The secret ingredient is your philosophy. The secret is to change the way you think. Once you do, then you will take the steps you need to take, to lead you to the how-to's you need. If you don't change your thinking, no amount of how-to's will offer a real solution. It's not the "hows," it's how you do the "hows."

This isn't about self-hypnosis, or about conjuring up the impossible through sheer positive thinking, or any other kind of hocus-pocus. And I'm not talking about some complex, elaborate or heady system of ideas. And—although I'll completely understand if you find the last part of this sentence truly difficult to believe—*what I'm talking about is not difficult to do.*

It simply means changing your thinking. Your philosophy.

The reason diets and other how-to's don't work for most people is the same reason most how-to books and courses don't work for most people. **It isn't that the actions are wrong. It's that people don't keep doing them.**

Focusing on the actions (the what-to-do's and the how-to-do it's) is not enough, because it's the attitude behind the actions that keeps those actions in place.

Aha! It's attitudes! So, what I need is an attitude adjustment ...

No, that won't necessarily do it either. Your emotions change. You can't dictate how you feel. No matter how much you may tell yourself to feel positive about this how-to step or that how-to step, what if you just don't? Today, you're excited about getting fit. You feel like doing your twenty minutes on the treadmill. Great! But what if tomorrow you just don't feel like doing it?

To find the path to success, you have to back up one more step. It's the understanding behind the attitudes that are behind the actions.

It's the philosophy. That's the secret ingredient. Your philosophy is what you know, how you hold it, and how it affects what you do. That's what this book is about.

Yes, you have to know the winning how-to actions, and you have to possess the winning attitudes—but what generates all that and keeps it all in place is your philosophy.

your **ATTITUDE**
your **ACTIONS**
your
PHILOSOPHY creates your **RESULTS** creates **LIFE**

A positive philosophy turns into a positive attitude, which turns into positive actions, which turn into positive results, which turn into a positive lifestyle.

A negative philosophy turns into a negative attitude, which turns into negative actions, which turn into negative results, which turn into a negative lifestyle.

Life Wisdom

What do I mean by philosophy? Not something lofty or abstract; not something you need to go to graduate school or learn Greek to understand. I mean something so simple, so basic, a six-year-old child can understand it.

Here is an example.

Do the thing, and you shall have the power.

— Ralph Waldo Emerson, *Compensation*

Profoundly simple and just as powerful. The sort of wisdom you can actually apply in everyday life. Nike simplified it for the MTV generation ("Just do it"), but I like the Emerson version better, and we'll be using it a good deal later on when we talk about applying the Slight Edge to your life.

There are two prevalent types of attitudes: entitled and value-driven. A value-driven attitude says, "What can I do to help you?" An entitled attitude says, "What have you done for me lately?" An entitled attitude says, "Pay me more, and then maybe I'll work harder." A value-driven attitude says, "I'll work harder, and then I expect you'll pay me more."

Which of these attitudes is driven by Emerson's philosophy, "Do the thing and you'll have the power"?

Your philosophy is *what you know, how you hold what you know, and how it affects what you do.* You can look at anyone's actions and trace back, through the attitudes behind those actions, to their source: the philosophy behind the attitudes. Show me what a man does, and I'll show you what his philosophy is.

Here's another example of a life philosophy:

> *The formula for success is quite simple:*
> *double your rate of failure.*
>
> — Thomas J. Watson, Sr. (founder of IBM)

We are not taught that the key to success is to "double your rate of failure." On the contrary, we're taught to avoid failure like the plague. "Failure is not an option!" Really? It had better be an option! It had better be, because whether or not you consider it an option, it's going to happen.

If you go through life with the philosophy that "failure is not an option," then you'll never have any good opportunities to learn. (Which won't really matter anyway, because if failing is not an option, chances are you won't even try in the first place!)

If Babe Ruth had had the philosophy, "Failure is not an option," then you and I would have never heard of him. Why? Because not only did Babe Ruth set a world record for home runs, he also led the league in strikeouts.

Michael Jordan, considered by many as one of the greatest basketball players of all time (winning six NBA titles with the Chicago Bulls), didn't make the varsity team as a sophomore because they thought he was too small. The next two years he grew four inches, honed his game … and the rest, as they say, is history.

Abraham Lincoln had an extraordinary record of lost elections and public-office failures over the course of his career. For the ungainly lawyer from Illinois, failure was not only an option, it was practically his specialty. If it hadn't been, he would never have made it to the White House.

And it's hard to imagine just what our lives would be like today if Thomas Edison had subscribed to the "Failure is not an option" philosophy. In his efforts to find a stable filament to make his electric light bulb invention work, he tried out thousands of different versions and every single one failed. His comment: "I have not failed. I've simply discovered ten thousand ways that don't work."

Successful people *fail* their way to the top!

The Slight Edge Philosophy

Your philosophy is your view of life, something beyond feelings and attitudes. Your philosophy drives your attitudes and feelings, which drive your actions.

By and large, people are looking in the wrong places. They are looking for a breakthrough, looking for that amazing "quantum leap"—the philosophy of the craps table and roulette wheel. I don't believe they'll ever find it. I've had colossal failures, and I've had remarkable successes, and my experience is, neither one happens in quantum leaps. They happen through the Slight Edge.

The purpose of this book is to have you understand the Slight Edge philosophy, to make it part of how you see the world and how you live your life every day. To understand patience; to understand that little steps, compounded, do make a difference. That the things you do every single day, the things that don't look dramatic, that don't even look like they matter, do matter. That they not only make a difference—they make all the difference.

Throughout this book, if you look carefully, you'll find at least a dozen statements (and if you look really closely, many dozens!) that embody this philosophy, statements such as "Do the thing, and you shall have the power." Here are a few more examples that you'll come across in the following pages:

Success is the progressive realization of a worthy ideal.

Successful people do what unsuccessful people are not willing to do.

There is a natural progression to everything in life: plant, cultivate, harvest.

Here's a suggestion that can maximize how much you get out of this book— that is, not only reading it, but also absorbing it and applying it in your life: every time you come to a fundamental statement of philosophy, highlight it. Then go back regularly and read through just those highlighted sections: your own personal guide to the Slight Edge philosophy.

The Slight Edge is also the philosophy embodied in the three stories you read in the beginning of this book. It is understanding the tremendous potential of something as seemingly insignificant as a penny. It is knowing how to recognize and harness the power of the water hyacinth. It's having faith in the process of simple, positive actions repeated over time, the faith that miracles do happen—if you know when to trust the process and keep churning the cream.

Just Add Life and Stir ...

The Slight Edge philosophy is the missing ingredient you need for all the personal-development books, how-to's and life guides to work.

If you don't grasp the truth of the Slight Edge, then no matter what health books you read, you're not going to be willing to do the little things that lead you to a healthy life. No matter what you learn, no matter how many books you read, CDs you listen to, or seminars you attend, if you don't absorb this philosophy of simple steps and their compounded effect over time, you won't successfully apply those things you learn to create the results you want.

The Slight Edge will help you apply all the information you learn from the health book, the sales book, the investment book, the positive attitude book. The Slight Edge is the book you need to read, highlight and reread along with your fitness class, your career planning, your continuing education and pursuit of new skills.

The Slight Edge will prepare you to be able to absorb all that other information, guidance and education from all those other books, classes, situations and experiences.

Whatever your deepest desires are in life, I want you to have them, and I know you can. That is my passionate belief—and I've seen it happen too many times to doubt it. But you need a place to start. The Slight Edge is that starting point. It's the first ingredient.

KEY POINTS OF CHAPTER 1

People everywhere are clamoring for the formula, the secret ingredient, the path to improve their lives. The secret ingredient is your philosophy: what you know, how you hold it and how it affects what you do. Once you change the way you think then you can take the steps that will lead you to the "how-to's."

The things you do every day, the things that don't look like they matter, do matter. They not only make a difference—they make all the difference.

Apply the Slight Edge Principles and Stir!

I have used the principles of the Slight Edge to improve my physical fitness, starting with one push-up and one sit-up a day, adding another each day and building to over 100 per day. I have used it to help pay off debt, build my savings and investments, and improve my relationships with my children.

— *Stan Snow, North Yarmouth, ME*

I have applied the Slight Edge principles in so many areas of life. Chunking every project into annual goals, monthly outcomes, weekly agendas and daily disciplines has helped me accomplish massive improvements in every area of life from health to relationships, to communication skills, to finances. By identifying the daily disciplines in every area of life, I was able to move from cancer to outstanding health; from non-communication with siblings to best friends; from struggling as a single mom to creating a net worth of over 1 million dollars! The Slight Edge principles, compounded over time, will make a massive shift in any area we choose.

—Linda Kedy, Destin, FL

By applying the principles of the Slight Edge, I've lost 35 pounds in just three months, and am still going strong. I'm also working the principles into my job, part-time pursuits and every area of my life. I have quit focusing as much on the goals, and am focusing more on the little things I do every day, since I can control those.

—Richard Green, Franklin, TN

After reading *The Slight Edge* I decided to apply the philosophies into every area of my life. As a father, I bought a copy for my kids and started imparting the wisdom of things that are easy to do/easy not to do. As a doctor, I started giving my patients who were dealing with hopelessness a copy of the book. I tell them it is Prozac in paperback. As an author, I implemented the Slight Edge principles into my books as well. For every role in your life there are Slight Edge applications that will make a huge difference!

—Baker Fore, Edmond, OK

CHAPTER 2

The Secret of Easy Things

'Tis a gift to be simple, 'tis a gift to be free,
'Tis a gift to come down where you ought to be,
And when we find ourselves in the place just right
'Twill be in the valley of love and delight.

— traditional Shaker hymn

Have you ever met a really successful person? You know whom I mean: that woman with the easy, engaging smile, the one who makes you feel instantly at ease, even as you stand in awe of her accomplishments. The guy who's always dressed for success, who looks great even when he isn't trying, and somehow makes you feel better about yourself just being in his presence. People who not only are successful, but also seem to breathe success and fill the space around them with it.

They live in beautiful homes, travel to exciting places, fly first class. Are surrounded by people who love them and admire them. Are appreciated, respected and recognized. Happy, healthy, creative and fulfilled. Winners in the game of life.

Why do some families have such great relationships, such warmth and fun and caring closeness, while others are perennially angry with each other, so distrustful and distant they might as well live on different planets? Why are some people positive and upbeat while others are miserably negative, constantly complaining and criticizing?

Why is it some people never seem to manage the time to stay in shape, while others run a few miles each day even though their lives are just as busy? Why are some people digging deeper and deeper into debt, while others just keep earning more money?

Why is it that some people seem to make dream after dream come true, while others spend their lives building someone else's dream? Why are some people successful, and some people failures?

What's the difference—really?

What Do Successful People Do?

You've probably read and heard lots of statistics. Happy versus unhappy marriages, health versus illness, how many retirees barely survive on fixed incomes versus how many reach their golden years in comfort and security. There are a hundred and one ways to measure it, but if you simply look around you, you can see it: most of us aren't making it.

My observation is that about one person in twenty is achieving a significant measure of his or her goals in life: financial, professional, personal, marital, spiritual, in terms of health, in whatever terms you want to look at. Ninety-five percent are either failing or falling short.

What are the five percent doing that the ninety-five percent are not?

There is only one difference. It is not heredity, education, looks, talent or inheritance. It is not "preparedness meeting opportunity," and it's not chance, either. They all understand the Slight Edge and how it is working for or against them.

If you will learn to understand and apply the Slight Edge, I will guarantee you that in time—and chances are, less time than you would imagine—you will have what you desire. You will be among the five percent. You will be successful. *And you will achieve those aims, goals and dreams by doing simple things.*

A bold claim, I know, and I make it only because I know it's true—I've seen it too many times to doubt it. If you learn to understand and apply the Slight Edge, your life will become filled with hundreds of thousands of small, seemingly insignificant actions—all of them easy to do, none of them mysterious, complex or difficult. And those actions will create your success.

That's what successful people do: simple things that are easy to do.

Simple Things

"Wait a minute. How are these simple, everyday actions supposed to create all this wonderful happiness, health and success for me, if they're all easy to do—if anyone could do them? If these are things anyone can do, why are only five percent successful?"

Excellent question. **Because they're all also easy not to do—and while anyone *could* do them, most *won't*.**

Fundamentally, we all take pretty much the same actions every day. We eat, sleep, think, feel, talk and listen. We have relationships and friendships. We each have twenty-four hours a day, 8,760 hours a year, and we each fill these hours one way or the other with a sequence of little tasks and actions, any one of which is seemingly insignificant.

Gold medal marathon runners eat and sleep. So do people who are thirty pounds overweight. Successful entrepreneurs think and feel and have relationships with other people. So do those who are unemployed or even living on the streets. People who make lots of money read books. People who are broke read books, too.

The successful and unsuccessful both do the same basic things in their lives, day in and day out. Yet the things successful people do take them to the top, while the things unsuccessful people do take them down and out.

So what's the difference? The difference is their awareness, understanding and use of the Slight Edge in their life and work.

Successful winners understand the Slight Edge.

Unsuccessful people do not.

The difference that will make *all* the difference between success and failure, between achieving the quality of life you want and settling for less than you desire and deserve, lies one hundred percent in which of those little, "insignificant" actions you choose to do. This is why we are all capable of doing what it takes to be successful. We are all capable of being winners ... and yes, that includes you.

The Slight Edge is always working. For you or against you, the Slight Edge is already, always at work in all our lives. The purpose of this book is to help you become aware of it—how it is working in your life, every day, every hour, every moment, in every step you take and every choice you make.

Easy to Do ... Easy Not to Do

Everything you need to do to transform your life is easy to do.

It's easy to become healthy, fit and vibrant. It's easy to become financially independent. It's easy to have a happy family and a life rich with meaningful friendships.

Tapping into the Slight Edge means doing things that are easy. Simple little disciplines that, done consistently over time, will add up to the very biggest accomplishments.

It's easy to have everything you ever wanted in your life. Every action you need to take to make any and all of your dreams come true is easy. So why is it, then, that the masses are unhappy, unhealthy and financially bound?

Every action that any of these goals requires is easy to do. **Here's the problem: every action that is easy to do, is also easy not to do.**

Why are these simple yet crucial things easy not to do? Because if you don't do them, they won't kill you ... at least, not today. You won't suffer, or fail or blow it—today. Something is easy not to do when it won't bankrupt you, destroy your career, ruin your relationships or wreck your health—today.

What's more, not doing it is usually more comfortable than doing it would be. But that simple, seemingly insignificant error in judgment, compounded over time, will kill you. It will destroy you and ruin your chances for success. You can count on it. It's the Slight Edge.

That's the choice you face every day, every hour: A simple, positive action, repeated over time. A simple error in judgment, repeated over time.

You can always count on the Slight Edge. And unless you make it work for you, the Slight Edge *will* work against you.

Invisible Results

If I could have had a magic wand that day in the Phoenix airport as I sat thinking and having my shoes shined, one of the first things I would have done would have been to wave it at the little pile of paperbacks. I would have waved the wand and *Presto!* Now there would be a little reading table piled with Napoleon Hill, James Allen, Stephen Covey and George S. Clason. Because the simple truth is, how you feed your mind is every bit as critical to your happiness as how you feed your body.

Seeing how naturally open-minded and intellectually curious the shoeshine woman was, I have no doubt she would have dove into any one of these books with gusto.

But then we would have run into a problem.

Everything you need to know to be successful—every how-to, every practical action—is already written in books like these. Here's a Slight Edge action guaranteed to change your life: read just ten pages of a good book, a book aimed at improving your life, every day.

If you read ten pages of a good book today, will your life change? Of course not. If you don't read ten pages of a good book today, will your life fall apart? Of course not.

I could tell my shoeshine friend that if she would agree to read ten pages of one of these good books every single day, over time, she could not help but accumulate all the knowledge she'd ever need to be as successful as she ever wanted to be—successful enough to send her daughter to that cheerleading camp and hey, to send her to the best college in the country if she wanted. Like a penny over time, reading ten pages a day would compound, just like that, and create a ten-million-dollar bank of knowledge in her.

Would she do it? On day 1, sure. And day 2. And maybe day 3. But would she still be doing it by the end of the week? If she did keep reading, over the course of the year she would have read 3,650 pages—the equivalent of one or two dozen books of life-transforming material! Would her life have changed? Absolutely. No question. But here, back in week 1, all that's still an *invisible result*.

And that is exactly why most people never learn to recognize or understand the Slight Edge, the reason most people never learn how to make the Slight Edge work for them, and why the Slight Edge ends up working against them:

When you make the right choice, you won't see the results. At least, not today.

We live in a result-focused world. We expect to see results, and we expect to see them now. Push the button, the light flicks on. Step on the scale, look in the mirror, check the account balance online 24/7. *Give me feedback, trip a sensor, hit a buzzer, tell me, tell me, tell me it's working!*

But that's not how success is built. **Success is the progressive realization of a worthy ideal.** "Progressive" means success is a process, not a destination. It's something you experience gradually, over time. Failure is also just as gradual. In fact, the difference between success and failure is so subtle, you can't even see it or recognize it during the process. And here's how real success is built: **by the time you get the feedback, the real work's already done.** When you get to the point where everyone else can see your results, tell you what good choices you've made, notice your good fortune, slap you on the back and tell you how lucky you are, the critical Slight Edge choices you made are ancient history. And chances are, at the time you actually made those choices, nobody noticed but you. And even you wouldn't have noticed—unless you understood the Slight Edge.

Invisible results.

The Cost of Waiting

I'm sure you've heard about the power of compounding interest before. In fact, you've probably heard about it many times. What makes this time different?

Nothing—unless you act on it.

The single most important thing I can tell you about the Slight Edge is this: it's already working, *right now*, either for you or against you. So don't wait.

My hope for you—my request for you—is that before you reach the last page of this book, you will have put in place a Slight Edge financial plan for yourself so that you are consistently building your equity. Some simple, daily (or weekly, or monthly) discipline that, over time, will buy your financial freedom.

Easy to do? Surprisingly so. Easy not to do? Tragically so.

To give you a sense of the cost of waiting, look at the following example.

Let's say you and your best friend are both twenty-four years old; you both read *The Slight Edge* and decide you'd like to start putting away $2,000 a year into an IRA so you'll retire at age sixty-five with over a million dollars.

Your friend starts doing it now. You wait. You don't get around to it this year, or next, or the next … in fact, you procrastinate for the next six years.

At the beginning of year 7, you ask your friend how his IRA is doing. You are stunned when he tells you that he's finished: after investing $2,000 a year for six years at twelve percent, he's all set. By the age of sixty-five, the little financial ball he's started rolling will have snowballed into over one million dollars—even if he never puts in another penny!

That's it, you decide, it's time for action. You start putting in your $2,000 each year. How many years will it take before you've caught up to your friend? In other words, by what age will you be able to stop investing your annual $2,000, like he did?

You can't believe your eyes when you see the answer: you're going to have to keep investing that $2,000 every single year until the age of sixty-two! **Your six years of procrastination has cost you thirty-three years of investing—that's twenty-seven more years and $54,000 more invested just to arrive at the same place!**

The Cost of Waiting

| | Your Friend | | | You | |
Age	Payment	Accum. Total	Payment	Accum. Total
24	$2,000	$2,240	0	0
25	2,000	4,749	0	0
26	2,000	7,559	0	0
27	2,000	10,706	0	0
28	2,000	14,230	0	0
29	2,000	18,178	0	0
30	0	20,359	$2,000	$2,240
31	0	22,803	2,000	4,749
32	0	25,539	2,000	7,559
33	0	28,603	2,000	10,706
34	0	32,036	2,000	14,230
35	0	35,880	2,000	18,178
36	0	40,186	2,000	22,599
37	0	45,008	2,000	27,551
38	0	50,409	2,000	33,097
39	0	56,458	2,000	39,309
40	0	63,233	2,000	46,266
41	0	70,821	2,000	54,058
42	0	79,320	2,000	62,785
43	0	88,838	2,000	72,559
44	0	99,499	2,000	83,507
45	0	111,438	2,000	95,767
46	0	124,811	2,000	109,499
47	0	139,788	2,000	124,879
48	0	156,563	2,000	142,105
49	0	175,351	2,000	161,397
50	0	196,393	2,000	183,005
51	0	219,960	2,000	207,206
52	0	246,355	2,000	234,310
53	0	275,917	2,000	264,668
54	0	309,028	2,000	298,668
55	0	346,111	2,000	336,748
56	0	387,644	2,000	379,398
57	0	434,161	2,000	427,166
58	0	486,261	2,000	480,665
59	0	544,612	2,000	540,585
60	0	609,966	2,000	607,695
61	0	683,162	2,000	682,859
62	0	765,141	2,000	767,042
63	0	856,958	0	861,327
64	0	959,793	0	966,926
65	0	$1,074,968	0	$1,085,197

"But what if I'm not twenty-four—what if I'm forty-four? Or sixty-four? Does that mean I've missed the boat—are you saying it's too late for me?"

Not at all. You're never too old, and it's never too late, to start applying Slight Edge tactics to achieve your dreams, financial and otherwise. In fact, best-selling author David Bach has written an excellent book titled *Start Late, Finish Rich*, addressing exactly that issue. Like all the other books I list in the Appendix, it's a great companion to *The Slight Edge*. My point is simply that there is a cost to waiting.

It's never too late to start.
It's always too late to wait.

Just ask Ramona B. Jenkins of Baltimore, a fan of *The Slight Edge*:

Before reading The Slight Edge, *money management wasn't one of my strong suits. After reading and re-reading the book several times, I began depositing a designated amount from each paycheck into a savings account, which soon became a compound interest-bearing account. It has been amazing to see the results of a simple decision to consistently save.*

I hope like Ramona you decide to make a Slight Edge commitment to your financial future.

What You Do Matters

I am as passionate about personal health and fitness as I am about financial health. I believe your health is your most prized possession. It amazes me how many people pay no attention to their health.

Do you know anyone who would eat a quart of Crisco or a pound of butter a day? *Hey, my cholesterol's down to 239, I need to get it up over 400. There are still a few arteries flowing and I need to get 'em all clogged, right now, today!* Does anyone believe that's the way to good health? Of course not. Then why do we act like we do?

You know what you're supposed to eat. We all do. Fresh fruits and vegetables, complex carbs, salads, whole foods, lean meats, more fish and poultry than beef ... You know it, I know it, we all know it. So why do so many of us still go out and chow down cheeseburgers and fries every day?

I'll tell you why: because it won't kill us. Not today.

If you ate a cheeseburger and immediately suffered a near-fatal heart attack, would you ever go near a cheeseburger again? I doubt it. It may take twenty or thirty years, but when you add up the compounded interest on all that high-fat, artery-clogging dietary mayhem, eventually your poor overworked heart just quits, stops dead. And so do you. It has been said that we dig our graves with our teeth.

It's easy to eat well. And it's easy not to.

It's not the one junk-food meal; it's the thousands, over time. Eating the burger is just a simple error in judgment. Not eating it, a simple positive action. Eating it won't kill you—today. But compounded over time, it can and will. Not eating it won't save you—today. But compounded over time, it can and will.

A simple, positive action. A simple error in judgment. Either way, it's the Slight Edge at work—working for you or working against you. For example, if you read 10 pages of a good book today will you see success? No. If you don't read 10 pages of a good book a day will you see failure? No. They look the same today.

Invisible results.

Why do you walk past the exercise bike? Because it's easy. If you don't exercise today, will that kill you? No, of course not. You know what you need to do to stay healthy and feel fit and live a long life. Get your heart rate up, a little over normal, for twenty minutes, three times a week. You know it, I know it, everyone knows it. And it's easy to do.

But it's also easy not to do. And if you don't do it today, or tomorrow, or the next day, you won't suddenly drop dead, and you won't suddenly put on twenty pounds, and you won't suddenly lose all your muscle tone and flop around like a marionette with his strings cut off. But that simple error in judgment, compounded over time, will take you down and out.

It is the same with your health, your diet, your exercise, your financial habits, your knowledge, your relationships, your marriage. With anything and everything. With your life.

You see one person eating a good meal, and the person next to him eating an awful meal. One person saving a penny, another spending a penny. One taking a brisk walk, another sitting and watching the news. Is there any difference between the two? Nothing you can see ... not today, and probably not tomorrow. It's easy to conclude that it doesn't really make any difference.

The difference between success and failure is not dramatic. In fact, the difference between success and failure is so subtle, most people miss it. They hold the philosophy that what they do doesn't really matter. It's not hard to see how people come to this understanding of life. I don't blame them. It's completely understandable. It's just not the truth.

The truth is, what you do matters. What you do today matters. What you do every day matters.

Successful people just do the things that seem to make no difference in the act of doing them and they do them over and over and over until the compound effect kicks in.

Those little things that will make you successful in life, that will secure your health, your happiness, your fulfillment, your dreams, are simple, subtle, tiny things that nobody will see, nobody will applaud, nobody will even notice. They are those things that, at the time you do them, often feel like they make absolutely no difference ... like they don't matter.

They do.

KEY POINTS OF CHAPTER 2

If you learn to understand and apply the Slight Edge, your life will become filled with hundreds of thousands of small, seemingly insignificant actions—all of them easy to do, none of them mysterious, complex or difficult. These are the actions that will create your success.

That's what successful people do: simple things that are easy to do. Here's the problem: every action that is easy to do, is also easy not to do. If you don't do them, you won't suffer, or fail or blow it—today. But that simple error in judgment, compounded over time will ruin your chances for success.

It's the Little Things That Matter

As an actress living in New York, it is so easy to get overwhelmed by everything that comes with this competitive business. *The Slight Edge* helped me to understand that the small choices I make every moment of every day make a huge impact on my life. Living in a society with so much emphasis on success, I found that *The Slight Edge* redefined what success is for me. It helps me to take the next step forward in my everyday life and do the next right thing. I know those steps will ultimately lead to a very successful and fulfilling life.

—*Cara Cooley, Spokane, WA*

We live in a world where we are bombarded by success tips. Some we apply, some we do not. *The Slight Edge* is a lifestyle to me, not a tip. It is a way of living that most fail to discover—especially now in this instant gratification world we live in. *The Slight Edge* is about doing key things that are easy to do and easy not to do. For me, my most important Slight Edge habit is ... looking for and finding something positive in every situation, no matter what.

Life experiences train us to see the negative, our shortcomings, and react to situations. To look for what we did wrong. It is just as easy to look for what we did well and build on that. Life gives us numerous opportunities to grow if we just see them for what they can mean.

Personally, reading and applying *The Slight Edge* daily has helped me ... lose over 60 pounds in 24 months, attract relationships with highly successful people who are now my mentors, develop self-confidence that grows every day, and so much more. Most of all, *The Slight Edge* has helped me clearly understand that investing just a few minutes a day to improve my life has a compounding affect. I now get up every day knowing that I am on the upward track to achieving my dream goals in all areas of my life ... and they are massive!

—Jim Hageman, Dallas, TX

I was in my second week of new program when I started reading *The Slight Edge*. Up until then I had been inconsistent in my workout routines and hadn't stuck with any program for more than a couple of weeks. They bore me. One night I went to bed late and told myself that I'd just skip my workout in the morning. The thought that went through my head was that it's the easy choices I make each day that make the difference in my success. With that thought, I got up the next morning and every morning after that. I'm now in the sixth week and I love my morning workouts. I look forward to them. Since I've never gotten this far, it is truly amazing how different I feel. I never thought I would look forward to working out.

—Laura Jo Richins, Mesa, AZ

CHAPTER 3

Is Time on Your Side?

Time is free, but it's priceless.
You can't own it, but you can use it.

You can't keep it but you can spend it.
Once you've lost it you can never get it back.

—Harvey Mackay

So you walk a little today, get your heart rate up a bit, you lift a few weights, you eat a little differently, then tomorrow morning you wake up and look in the mirror ... and see the same old flubber. You have to be pretty well along the path to see any significant results. What keeps you doing this simple thing, day after day?

Will power! It's like my dad (mom, teacher, boss, older brother, minister, self) always told me ... I just need more will power.

Really? I don't think so. (A friend of mine used to say that people on diets who complain that they lack will power are usually suffering more from a lack of won't power!) Will power is vastly overrated. For most people, will power ends up looking and feeling like some sort of grim self-tyranny, and involves creating an elaborate, artificial reward-and-punishment system.

Do you want to change? If so, I can show you how to tap into the most powerful force for change there is. Would you like to know what it is? Are you ready? Here it is:

TIME.

Position your daily actions so time is working for instead of against you. Because time will either promote you or expose you.

What keeps you on the path is your Slight Edge philosophy, which includes your understanding of the secret of time. Knowing the secret of time, you say, *If I stay on this road long enough, I'll get the result I seek.* It's not a question of your mood or your feelings. And it's not a question of will power. It's a question of simply *knowing.*

When you enter a darkened room, why does your hand reach out for the light switch? Because you know that when you hit the switch, the light will go on. You don't have to give yourself positive self-talk about how you really ought to hit that light switch, or set up a system of rewards and punishments for yourself around whether you follow through or not with hitting the light switch. You don't need any rigmarole; you just hit the switch. Why? Because you know what will happen.

You *know.*

It's the exact same thing here: you walk a little every day, lift a few weights, eat a little better, and leave the penny in the purse (hit the light switch) because you know it will make you healthy and wealthy (the light will turn on).

It's the exact same thing, no different—except for one thing, and that is time.

"Instant Life"

If you were offered the same choice the wealthy man gave his sons, would you choose the million dollars or the penny? Most people would make the second boy's choice: the right-now money—the quantum leap. After all, a million dollars! In cash! Right now!

And, of course, you'd be making the wrong choice—and you would have been fooled, as millions of people around the globe are fooled every minute of every hour of every day, by those two seductive little words:

Right now!

I remember one day seeing a man standing in front of a microwave, fidgeting impatiently as he peered through the window at his lunch being cooked, and muttering, "Come onnnn ... come onnnn ... !"

It blew my mind. Sixty seconds wasn't fast enough?!

It's become a truism to say we live in a push-button, instant-access, fast-food kind of world where we want everything yesterday.

This doesn't mean we have more impatient temperaments than our parents did. It represents an entirely different way of thinking. An entirely different philosophy.

There is a natural progression in life, which everyone knew intimately back in the days when we were an agrarian society. **You plant, then you cultivate, and finally you harvest. Plant, cultivate, harvest.**

In today's world, everyone wants to go directly from plant to harvest. We plant the seed by joining the gym, and then get frustrated when a few days go by and there's no fitness harvest. Taking recreational drugs is an effort to go from plant directly to harvest. So is taking steroids to enhance athletic performance. So is robbing a bank; so is playing the lottery.

The step we keep overlooking (and overskipping!) is the step of cultivating. And that, unlike planting and harvesting, takes place only through the patient dimension of time.

Because we are a culture raised on television and movies, we've lost track of time. We don't understand time any more. I'm not criticizing television and films. Film is an amazing art form, television is a powerful medium, and in the hands of true artists, they can both teach us valuable lessons about life. Just not about time.

Through a great film, you can experience the triumph of the human soul over adversity, the drama of a struggle between doing what's right and succumbing to the temptations of the world, a moving encounter between generations, the flowering of a powerful romance, the struggle and birth of a nation ...

But it all has to be finished in *two hours*.

Can you imagine a nation being born in two hours? Meeting the person who will become the love of your life—the dating, courtship, romance, struggle, triumph, wedding and life thereafter—in two hours? Of course not. We expect to put forth the effort of a short "training sequence" in a movie and get the same heroic ending. In a world filled with instant coffee, instant breakfast, instant credit, instant shopping, instant news and instant information, **we have come dangerously close to losing touch with reality and believing we have access to *instant life*.**

Where's the Drama?

It's not that becoming aware of the Slight Edge will make these critical choices easier—because they're already easy! And that, oddly enough, is the challenge of it. This is not about making tough choices. It's about making easy choices consistently.

The problem is, making the wrong choices—the ones that will tilt the Slight Edge to lean against you instead of in your favor—are also easy choices.

In a way, it would be a simpler matter if making the right choices were a big deal. If it were a dramatic, huge, difficult thing. Why? Because then it would be obvious. You wouldn't need this book. The challenge is that making the right choices is not dramatic. When the hero makes the right choice in a movie, it's dramatic, all right. Problem is, your life is not a movie. It's real life.

Deciding whether or not to kill Darth Vader with your light saber is a dramatic choice. Deciding whether or not to fasten your seat belt is an undramatic, boring, mundane little choice that nobody will even witness. But guess which choice has the power to take a few hundred thousand lives each year? Hint: it's not the light saber.

If making the right Slight Edge choices were a dramatic thing, you'd get *immediate feedback*. An entire movie theater audience applauding, cheering or screaming. But that doesn't happen. And that's the big challenge of it: no immediate feedback.

The right choices and wrong choices you make at the moment will have little or no noticeable impact on how your day goes for you. Nor tomorrow, nor the next day. No applause, no cheers, no screams, no life-or-death results played out in Technicolor. But it is precisely those very same, undramatic, seemingly insignificant actions that, when compounded over time, will *dramatically* affect how your life turns out.

So, where's the drama? It comes at the end of the story, when the credits start to roll—which comes not in two hours but in two years. Or, depending on what Slight Edge and what particular story we're talking about, perhaps twelve years, or twenty-two.

Making the right choices, taking the right actions. It's truly easy to do. Ridiculously easy. But it's just as easy not to do. And if you don't do them, there won't be any big drama about it. It won't kill you; it won't hurt you; in fact, it won't make any difference at all ...

Not today, anyway. Not tomorrow. But over time?

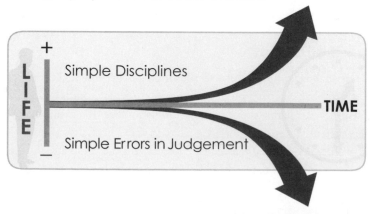

The right choices you make today, compounded over time, will take you higher and higher up the success curve of this real-time movie called "your life." The wrong choices you make today, compounded over time, will absolutely, positively and inevitably *take you down and out.*

Either way, there *will* be dramatic results, just like in a movie. Unlike a movie, it will just take time before you see them.

Jerry Sanchez, of El Paso, Texas understands fully that making the right choices daily can add up to good things:

> *After reading* The Slight Edge, *I decided to apply it to business (my job). I didn't do anything drastic, or make any major changes in my life. I simply began to read 10 pages of a good book per day. I also started to think before I made a decision. I would ask myself, Is this decision going to help me or hurt me? It was the day-to-day decisions that transformed everything in my life. After a year and a half of putting this in place, I got the position I always wanted at work, and an increase of $12,000 a year.*
>
> *I had worked for the company six years before putting the principles of* The Slight Edge *in place. The greatest joy was when my boss called me into his office, and said that I had changed over the last two years. I told him that I didn't notice, and he told me that everyone else had!*

Making the Choice to Make the Choice

For twenty-one years, the wealthy man gave his sons everything he had, including all his love, all his care and a magnificent place to live. But when they turned twenty-one, he gave them the most valuable gift of all. He gave them a choice.

That most valuable gift of all is a gift that you always have. You always have a choice.

No matter what you have done in your life up until today, no matter where you are and how far down you may have slid on the failure curve, you can start fresh, building a positive pattern of success, at any time. Including right now.

But you need to have faith in the process, because *you won't see it happening at first.*

If you base your choices on the evidence, on what you can see, you're sunk. You need to base your choices on your philosophy   on what you know, not what you see.

The Slight Edge is like Lady Justice, the famous blindfolded statue. The statue itself, of the woman holding the scales and sword, has been around since the days of ancient Rome. The blindfold was added in the sixteenth century, in the years leading up to that era we call the "Enlightenment" that gave birth to modern ideas of representative democracy and universal human rights. The blindfold is not meant to signify that justice is "blind," as people sometimes assume, but that true justice is impervious to external influence.

That also makes it a very good representation of the Slight Edge.

If you want to understand and apply the Slight Edge to create the life of your dreams, you can't make your choices based on the evidence of your eyes. You need to make them based on what you know. On your philosophy.

Picture success and failure as the two sides of a pair of balance scales, like the one held by Lady Justice.

Let's say you're in a tough place in your life. The scales are tipped badly, the negative side tilted way down. Whether it's your health, or your finances, or your marriage, or your career ... whatever it is, you've reached a place where many years of simple errors in judgment have compounded over time, and you're feeling it. You're behind the eight ball. It sure would be nice if, somehow, you could do something dramatic. If you just wake up tomorrow and have it all turned around—snap your fingers and change it.

That might happen, in a movie. But this is your life. What can you do?

What happens if you add one small, simple, positive action to the success side? Nothing you can see. What happens if you add one more? Nothing you can see. What happens if you keep adding one more, and one more, and one more, and one more ...

Before too long, you see the scales shift, ever so slightly. And then again. And eventually, that heavy "failure" side starts to lift, and lift, and lift ... and the scales start swinging your way. No matter how much negative weight from the past is on the other side, just by adding those little grams of success, one at a time (and by not adding more weight to the failure side), you will eventually and inevitably begin to shift the scales in your favor.

Way back in the beginning, when you add the first few morsels of positive action, if you judge your choices by the evidence of your eyes, you won't see the scales move at all and that will frustrate you. It frustrates nineteen out of twenty people so much, they quit. And that is the saddest thing I can think of.

The Power of Compounding Effort

Picture a huge, heavy flywheel—a massive metal disk mounted horizontally on an axle, about thirty feet in diameter, two feet thick, and weighing about 5,000 pounds. Now imagine that your task is to get the flywheel rotating on the axle as fast and for as long as possible.

Pushing with great effort, you get the flywheel to inch forward, moving almost imperceptibly at first. You keep pushing and, after two or three hours of persistent effort, you get the flywheel to complete one entire turn.

You keep pushing, and the flywheel begins to move a bit faster, and with continued great effort, you move it through a second rotation. You keep pushing in a consistent direction. Three turns ... four ... five ... six ... the flywheel builds up speed ... seven ... eight ... you keep pushing ... nine ... ten ... it builds momentum ... eleven ... twelve ... moving faster with each turn ... twenty ... thirty ... fifty... a hundred.

Then at some point—breakthrough! The momentum of the thing kicks in your favor, hurling the flywheel forward, turn after turn ... whoosh! ... its own heavy weight working for you. You're pushing no harder than the first rotation, but the flywheel goes faster and faster. Each turn of the flywheel builds upon work done earlier, compounding your investment of effort. A thousand times faster, then ten thousand, then a hundred thousand. The huge heavy disk flies forward with almost unstoppable momentum.

Now suppose someone came along and asked, "What was the one big push that caused this thing to go so fast?"

You wouldn't be able to answer; it's a nonsensical question. Was it the first push? The second? The fifth? The hundredth? No! It was all of them added together in an overall accumulation of effort applied in a consistent direction. Some pushes may have been bigger than others, but any single heave—no matter how large—reflects a small fraction of the entire cumulative effect upon the flywheel.

—From *Good to Great: Why Some Companies Make the Leap ... and Others Don't*, by Jim Collins

Successful people do whatever it takes to get the job done, whether or not they feel like it. They understand that it is not any one single push on the flywheel, but the cumulative total of all their sequential, unfailingly consistent pushes that eventually creates movement of such astonishing momentum in their lives.

Successful people form habits that feed their success, instead of habits that feed their failure. They choose to have the Slight Edge working for them, not against them. They build their own dreams, rather than spend their lives building other people's dreams, and they achieve these dramatic results in their lives through making choices that are the very antithesis of drama—mundane, simple, seemingly insignificant choices.

Every decision you make is a Slight Edge decision. What you're going to do, how you're going to act, what you're going to read, who you're going to chat with on the phone, what you're going to eat for lunch, who you're going to associate with. How you're going to treat your fellow workers. What you're going to get done today.

Simply by making those right decisions, or making more of them—one at a time, over and over again—you will have enlisted the awesome power of the Slight Edge on your behalf. The unwanted circumstances, the poor results you've produced in the past, and the evidence of failures in your life, may all continue for a time. There may be no light at the end of the tunnel, or at least none you can see today. But **by putting time on your side, you've marshaled the forces of the Slight Edge. Your success becomes inevitable. You just need to stay in the process long enough to give it a chance to win.**

It starts with a choice.

Cultivating Patience

Patience is a challenge for people who do not understand the Slight Edge.

Often, in the beginning, the success path can be uncomfortable, even scary. Especially if you're the only one around who's on it. And with only one out of twenty people ever achieving their goals, it's quite likely that you *will* be the only one around on the path—at least for a while.

Sometimes the path of success is inconvenient, and therefore easier not to do. For most people, it's easier to stay in bed. Getting on the path and staying on the path requires faith in the process—especially at the start. That makes you a pioneer.

Pioneers don't know what's out there, but out there, they go anyway. That's why being a pioneer takes such courage. *Courage* means to have a purpose and to have heart. Once you are aware of and understand how to use the Slight Edge, you will naturally have both—purpose and the strength of heart to stay on that purpose.

The important point is to start on the path and to remember that no matter what has gone on before, you can begin fresh and new and at any time you can choose to start with a clean slate.

How long will it take? How long before you will actually see and feel (and smell and touch and be able to spend and enjoy and appreciate) the results? How long before you will have the experience of the success you're seeking?

Obviously, it's impossible for either of us to say exactly how long. But the truth is, in three to five years, you can put virtually anything in your life onto the right track. Think of what you were doing three years ago: it seems like yesterday, doesn't it? Well, three years from now, the things you're doing right now will seem like only yesterday, too. Yet this brief little period of time can change your life.

How long will it take? Chances are it will take longer than you want it to ... and when the time arrives, you'll be astonished at how quick it seemed.

Patience is not an issue for the water hyacinth. It simply goes about its business, calmly, quietly doubling, until it covers the pond. You can do the same.

Serene, I fold my hands and wait,
Nor care for wind, nor tide, nor sea;
I rave no more 'gainst time or fate,
For lo! my own shall come to me.

—John Burroughs, *Waiting*

The Slight Edge guarantees that *your own shall come to you*, like the water hyacinth covering the pond. The way your own shows up, good or bad, failure or success, win or lose, is, moment by moment, up to you. You need not "care for wind, or tide, or sea ..."—but you do need to care for those simple little actions which, compounded over time, will make the difference between your success or failure.

The problem is that most of us live with one foot planted firmly in the past and the other tucked timidly in the future—never in the moment. In relation to everything—our kids, our health, our home, our career—we tick through the hours in constant regret and Monday-morning-quarterbacking about what's behind us, and with worry, anxiety and dread about what lies ahead.

The Slight Edge is all about living in the moment. For me personally, it is perhaps the hardest lesson to learn about the Slight Edge: you can't find it in the past or the future, only right here, right now.

The reason Ekhart Tolle's modest little 1997 book on enlightenment, *The Power of Now*, took the marketplace by storm, selling over two million copies in thirty languages, is that his core message is one that everyone knows they need to hear: *your life exists only in the moment.* But you can't really absorb or live that truth through reading a book; you absorb and live that truth simply by being fully in the process of living your life—not regretting the past, not dreading the future.

The Slight Edge is about your awareness. It is about you making the right choices, the choices that serve you and empower you, starting right now and continuing for the rest of your life, and learning to make them effortlessly.

This book is about putting the Slight Edge to work for you, instead of against you.

It's easy to do. And it's easy not to do. And if you don't do it, it won't kill you or destroy your chances for success today. But that simple error in judgment, compounded over time, will kill your chances for success. It will take you down and out of your life forever. And that choice is always yours.

The choice of simple things, and the wisdom to make that choice. The wealthy man was right: the third gift is one that you can only claim; it's something nobody can give you.

It's also something no one can take *away* from you.

KEY POINTS OF CHAPTER 3

The most powerful force for change is time. Position your daily actions so time is working for instead of against you. Because time will either promote you or expose you. What keeps you on the path is your Slight Edge philosophy which includes your understanding of the secret of time. Knowing that if I stay on this path long enough I will get the results I want.

In today's world, everyone wants to go directly from plant to harvest. The step we keep overlooking is the step of cultivating. And that, unlike planting and harvesting, takes place only through the patient dimension of time. The right choices you make today, compounded over time, will take you higher up the success curve.

Success Is Not a Race, It's a Journey

For many years I wanted to be my own boss, and when the opportunity presented itself I started my first business. Unfortunately, after a few years the business failed and I lost everything. It was a pretty demoralizing experience and one that I liked to deny responsibility for. Shortly afterwards I was given a audio copy of *The Slight Edge* and my eyes were opened. Although it seemed like my business had failed overnight, when I really thought about it nothing could have been further from the truth. For a long time I had been applying the Slight Edge in reverse, and the cumulative effect of that, as I found out, is devastating.

I'm happy to say that since then I have been applying Slight Edge principles in the correct manner, and although it has taken awhile (no one said it would be easy, did they?) things are now moving forward in a very positive direction. I have a beautiful wife, a lovely family, and my first children's book is being published this month, with a series of 12 planned over the next two years. The future for our family looks extremely bright, and I know from the bottom of my heart that this is down to consistent application of the Slight Edge.

—*Mark Hibbitts, Author of* Alfie Potts™ the Schoolboy Entrepreneur

I grew up in a middle class family where I was taught to go to school, get good grades and get a good job. Unfortunately my plan was derailed by some family medical circumstances that I could not control. At the age of 21 I found myself making $4.25 per hour working six days a week pursuing the philosophies of my parents.

The Slight Edge opened my mind to new horizons as I realized my past did not have to equal my future. I now knew that with a slight change in activity and consistency it was only a matter of time before I reached my true destiny. With these changes I created a six-figure income by the age of 30 and today I am a millionaire with five wonderful children and a beautiful wife to spend the rest of my life with. No matter what circumstances you find yourself in, by applying the Slight Edge principles over time you can positively change the trajectory of your life.

—*Dave Hall, Highland, UT*

CHAPTER 4

You Have to Start with a Penny

A journey of a thousand miles begins with a small step.
— Lao Tzu

I've presented the story of the penny doubled every day to hundreds and hundreds of audiences, and often I hear a comment like this:

Wow, that's amazing ... to think that you could start with nothing and build a fortune!

That's not quite accurate: **you don't start with nothing. You start with a penny.**

No big deal, I mean, of course, you start with a penny, but, you know, it's basically starting with nothing.

No, it's not: it's starting with a penny. It may seem like an insignificant difference (although you're probably starting to have a little bit different view of the word "insignificant"). The truth is, it makes *all* the difference.

To accomplish anything worth accomplishing, to create success, to achieve your dreams, you don't have to do impossible, extraordinary, superhuman things. But you have to do *something*. You have to start with a penny.

Success doesn't come from nowhere; it can't be conjured up out of thin air. It comes from a very small, tiny beginning—but there has to be a beginning. That beginning is the thing people miss, the thing they don't see. And they don't see it because it's so tiny, it's almost invisible.

Some of the largest companies in the world started out as nothing. Take Facebook, for example. Mark Zuckerberg started with just a concept—a penny—in his small Harvard dorm room, and today it has become the largest social networking site on the Internet, with over half a billion users. But in the beginning stages, when it was just a penny, Mark Zuckerberg believed in it enough to continue to take consistent action in building his vision, no matter if people believed in his penny or not.

A dead-broke, struggling young English teacher named Steve had started writing a story about a troubled high-school girl. Within a handful of pages, he realized the story wasn't working out and tossed the pages in the trash. Why add yet one more to his large and growing stack of rejection notices?

The next day, as Steve's wife was doing some straightening up, she bent down to empty his trash basket and happened to notice the curled little sheaf of papers. She straightened them out, dusted off the cigarette ashes, read them and took them to Steve: she thought he maybe had something worth finishing.

She was right. He did finish it, and the paperback rights sold for nearly a half a million dollars. What's more, his story of the troubled school girl named Carrie launched Stephen King's career: he became the most successful writer in the twentieth century.

What Tabitha King recognized in the trash may have been a tarnished penny, but still, it was a penny.

One chilly day in December 1955, an unknown forty-two-year-old seamstress in Montgomery, Alabama, decided she'd had enough. She was tired after a long day's work. Most of all, she was tired of being treated the way she was—and tired of every other person of her color being treated that way, too. So when she was told to give up her bus seat to a white passenger, she refused—even when the bus driver threatened her with arrest.

It was no idle threat; she was arrested, then convicted and fined for violating a city ordinance. Her case was the catalyst for the formation of a new civil rights organization. On the same day of the woman's hearing, the newly formed Montgomery Improvement Association elected a young and relatively unknown minister named Martin Luther King Jr. to be its spokesperson, launching a movement that over the next decade abolished legal segregation and radically transformed the face of the nation.

Rosa Parks was a penny.

The Slight Edge reader James Paris of Daytona Beach, Florida, knows the power of the penny.

> *Six years ago I learned that my accountant had embezzled $2 million from our company. I ended up in bankruptcy and languished in depression for five years. About six months ago I purchased* The Slight Edge *and I was able to find the motivation to just take a small step every day toward rebuilding my life.*
>
> *Now I am back on TV and radio and writing again. I have rebuilt my website ChristianMoney.com and have had multiple financial breakthroughs. I realized that I could not change my past but that I could rebuild a new future by taking just a small step every day in the right direction, just like the power of the penny. In just a few months I am well on the way to regaining the success I had prior to losing everything.*

Let's do one more bit of time travel. There was a time, a certain number of years ago, when a tiny blob of gelatin began to pulse with hidden potential. It was barely more than a speck of matter, about the thickness of a dollar bill, at the very threshold of human sight: any smaller and it would have been invisible to the naked eye.

Though tiny, this insignificant little dot of matter (you could have fit about twenty of them on the head of a pin) contained chemical instructions that, if printed out, would have filled more than 500,000 pages; in fact, it was among the most organized, complex structures in the universe. Over the next nine months of Slight Edge compounding, this little blob of gelatin would blossom into over thirty trillion cells before being born into the open air ... and letting out a wail as it took its first breath.

It would become you.

You started as a penny.

A Penny for Your Thoughts ...

Now imagine that instead of a penny doubling every day, it's your health that you're increasing by one penny's worth ... and then by two pennies, and then four.

If you could come up with something that would make you feel one penny's worth better, could you do that every day? Of course. A little moderate exercise, a brisk one-mile walk, a quarter of an hour on a treadmill, not going that fast. Get your heart rate up slightly, no big deal.

And your reward? When you get up the next morning, do you feel better?

Not really. I mean, not noticeably. Maybe just a little ... say, a penny's worth. Hardly seems worth the effort. And after a week, you're feeling sixty-four cents' worth better. Big deal! You've had to put up with some rainy weather, walk through a few stiff muscles, and miss your favorite news program ... hey, it's really not worth it.

But what if you kept doing it anyway? Would you eventually feel like a million bucks? No—you'd feel like *ten* million.

But you need to start with the penny.

Now imagine that penny is your knowledge.

If I told you that reading Napoleon Hill's *Think and Grow Rich* would change your life, would you sit down and read it, cover to cover, today? Mind you, that's a 256-page book, and those aren't lightweight pages. Or another classic, Stephen Covey's *The 7 Habits of Highly Effective People*. That's a 358-pager, and it's not easy reading.

Would you read either one in a single day? I doubt it. I wouldn't—I can't spend the entire day reading, and I'll bet you can't either.

But could you read a penny's worth—say, ten pages? (Actually, at current used-book prices on amazon.com, ten pages of the Hill book would cost about fifty cents, and ten pages of the Covey book would run about ten cents—but I'm using the penny here as a metaphor!) I don't know how much you would get out of ten pages; maybe a lot, maybe nothing. Let's say you get nothing. But if you could read ten pages today, could you read ten more tomorrow? Of course you could—anyone who can read could do that.

And if you do that, and you keep it up every day for a year, you will have read about a dozen brilliant, life-transforming classics. Your mind will be filled with the strategies and know-how to create a startling new level of success. You will have thoughts of millionaires—all from a penny.

But you need to start with the penny.

Let's Get Real

"Okay, doubling a penny in a story is all very well. But I don't see anyone offering to double my money every day for a month, not in real life. Besides, even if I could get compound interest on a money account, how am I supposed to add up compound interest in health, or relationships, or knowledge?"

Fair enough. Let's change the question. Forget about doubling for a minute, and let's forget about compound interest, too, for the moment. Let's just *add a penny* every day, not double the penny. Do you think you could improve yourself—your health, your knowledge, your skills, your diet, your relationships, whatever area of life you want to look at—just one percent?

Wait—before you answer that, let's make it even smaller. What if you were able to improve yourself, today, just *three-tenths* of one percent? That's a 0.003 improvement—a very Slight Edge indeed. So slight, in fact, you might have a hard time even knowing how to measure it.

Now, what if you did that again tomorrow, and the next day, and kept it up every day for the next year? Remember, you're not going to add up compound interest this time, you're just adding on another three-tenths of one percent each day.

Here's what will happen. The first day you'll improve by 0.003, so little it will probably be impossible to notice. The second day, your improvement will be 0.006; the next day, 0.009, almost a full one percent. And by the end of the year, you will have improved by one hundred percent.

Doubled.

You will be *twice* what you are today—twice as fit, twice as wealthy, twice as skilled, twice as happy ... twice as whatever it is you've been working on, in whatever areas **you apply your daily three-tenths-percent effort**. Twice the *you*, in just one year!

If you give yourself a year to do it, you can become twice the person you are today. Imagine having twice the net worth, twice the personal relationships, twice the health. Making twice the positive impact on the world. Having twice as much fun and enjoying twice the quality of life.

How could you possibly accomplish this? By trying twice as hard? Working twice as many hours? Have double the positive attitude? No—by improving three-tenths of one percent at a time.

Every day, in every moment, you get to exercise choices that will determine whether or not you will become a great person, living a great life. Greatness is not something predetermined, predestined or carved into your fate by forces beyond your control. **Greatness is always in the moment of the decision**.

But you have to start with a penny. And that's the great and tragic irony of it, the sad and terrible tale of the ninety-five percent: that little penny seems so insignificant, so small, so silly ... why even bother to bend over and pick it up? After all ...

Can you imagine walking into your bank to deposit a single penny into a savings account? Can you imagine looking in your savings account, deposit box or piggy bank, and finding a balance of $0.01? It might as well be a balance of zero, right? How much difference is there, right? I mean, we're talking about one penny! What could you buy with a penny?

KEY POINTS OF CHAPTER 4

To accomplish anything worth accomplishing, to create success, to achieve your dreams, you don't have to do impossible, extraordinary, superhuman things. But you have to do something. You have to start with a penny. Do you think you could improve yourself—your health, your knowledge, your skills, your diet, your relationships, whatever area of life you want to look at—just one percent?

The Power of the Penny

Read how these *The Slight Edge* readers started with a penny and ended up accomplishing amazing things.

My husband was an undercover narcotics officer in Chicago. He had a horrible accident at work when he was hit by a semi. This ended his career at 39. The main artery to his heart burst, he lost a lung, liver and his kidneys failed, he was in a coma for six weeks and spent seven months on life support. He came home after a year, in a wheelchair and on oxygen. There began a journey that God put me on. The following year we had no income as we waited for his disability hearings to complete. We nearly lost our home and were up to our ears in debt to everyone, everywhere. We were living the Slight Edge as we worked our way through small accomplishments, like just standing for three seconds and noting this on a calendar, going without oxygen for a minute, noting that, etc., until he made a miraculous recovery, which even his doctors and nurses are amazed at. This is the Slight Edge and the power of starting with a penny at its best.

—Lynn Lionhood, Orland Park, IL

My daughter had health complications a few years back, which left her on six or seven different medications. These of course created severe weight gain. After reading *The Slight Edge*, I suggested that she ride her stationary bike every day to help her drop some weight. At first she could only do 3 minutes, then 5 then 8 and so on. Eventually she progressed up to 20 minutes. After a year, it seemed like, all of a sudden, my daughter lost 25 pounds and we are all in shock, wondering what is happening. It took me a moment, but then I realized it was the power of the Slight Edge, 15 minutes a day.

—Valerie Thomas, Yeadon, PA

After suffering a stroke, Al Lewis of Illinois looked to lessons he learned from *The Slight Edge* to prove his doctor's initial diagnosis that he would probably never walk again wrong. When Al started his recovery process he could barely move and had lost the ability to speak. He knew if he wanted to get back to the life he enjoyed before the stroke he would have to stay focused on improving a tiny bit each day, and not get bogged down in his current circumstances. Here is an excerpt from what Al Lewis shared with *The Loyola Living Medical Journal*, where he was featured for his impressive recovery.

The Slight Edge taught me that if you do a little bit each day, a little bit, a little bit, you can make progress, great progress. I applied that philosophy to my rehabilitation. I started moving my fingers, a little bit. Then my hand, and then my arm a little bit. Now I go bike riding and I spend 30 minutes on an elliptical trainer. It all starts with just a little bit. Now my doctors tell me that although half of patients with my kind of stroke don't survive, when they look at me they can't event tell I have had a stroke. I had faith throughout the entire rehabilitation process that if I could just improve .003 percent each day compounded over time, I would make a full recovery.

Today Al has made a full recovery, including walking and talking, and has been able to return to his passions of playing music and speaking to audiences. Al serves as a shining example for all of us to look past our current circumstances and to focus on where we want to go by improving little by little.

CHAPTER 5

The Quantum Leap Myth

Some Day ...

Some day, when my ship comes in ...
Some day, when I have the money ...
Some day, when I have the time ...
Some day, when I have the skill, the confidence ...

How many of those statements have you said to yourself? **Have I got some shocking news for you: "some day" doesn't exist, never has, and never will. There is no "some day." There's only today.** When tomorrow comes, it will be another today; so will the next day. They all will. There is never anything but today.

And some more shocking news: your ship's not coming—it's already here. Docked and waiting. You already have the money. You already have the time. You already have the skill, the confidence. You already have everything you need to achieve everything you want.

You just can't see it.

Why not? Because you're looking in the wrong place. You're looking for the breakthrough, the quantum leap. **You're looking for the winning lottery ticket in a game that isn't a lottery!**

Have you ever noticed that when you read stories about lottery winners, they are hardly ever bank presidents, successful entrepreneurs or corporate executives? That they never seem to be people who were *already* financially successful before they bought that winning ticket? Have you ever wondered why? It's because successful people never win the lottery. Why not? Because they don't buy lottery tickets.

Successful people have already grasped the truth that lottery players have not: life is not a lottery. Success is not a random accident.

Greek Gods and Real Heroes

In ancient Greek theater, characters generally got themselves into as much of a mess as the playwright could possibly dream up. Everything would be headed for an absolutely impossible disaster when (in the last few minutes of the play) an actor playing a "god" would come floating down from the sky to make everything right—banishing this character and reinstating that one, punishing another and granting divine clemency to still another, explaining the inexplicable and solving the insoluble.

Things would be in such a mess, there'd be no way a human being could sort the stuff out. Obviously, it would have to take a being with divine powers. And just like in a stage production of *Peter Pan*, the actor would be suspended by ropes and a system of pulleys, a mechanical contrivance they termed a "machine," or *machina*.

Today, thousands of years later, people still refer to a last-minute "cheat" solution for an impossible problem coming out of thin air as a *deus ex machina,* or "god dropping in out of nowhere by a machine"—the supernatural, breakthrough force that pops in just to make all things right. And by the way, when critics say a play, novel or film uses a *"deus ex machina,"* it's not a compliment! It's their way of saying, "Oh yeah, right. Couldn't come up with a real solution, huh, so you had to trot in a *deus ex machina*? Gimme a break!"

And that is just what it is people are hoping for: a break. The big break. The lucky break. The breakthrough. A break in the routine ... a break with reality. A *deus ex machina*. But that's not how things really work.

Okay, then, how do things really work?

Look at some of the real-world problems that would have made Athena or Apollo or any other deity of Greek drama pull their hair out.

William Wilberforce spent his entire career introducing bill after bill to his colleagues in the British Parliament in his efforts to end slavery, only to have them defeated one after the other. From 1788 to 1806, he introduced a new anti-slavery motion and watched it fail every single year for eighteen years in a row. Finally, three days before Wilberforce's death in 1833, Parliament passed a bill to abolish slavery not only in England but also throughout its colonies. Three decades later, a similar bill would pass in the United States (spearheaded by another man of conscience who had also spent much of his life failing): Abraham Lincoln's Emancipation Proclamation.

Deus ex machina? Far from it. These were human problems, and they had human solutions. But the only access to them is through the Slight Edge.

Of course, Wilberforce and Lincoln were not the sole figures in this heroic struggle, and even after their bills were passed into law on both sides of the Atlantic, the evils of slavery and racism were far from over. But their efforts—like Mother Teresa's efforts to end poverty, Gandhi's to end colonial oppression, or Martin Luther King's and Nelson Mandela's to end racism—are classic examples of what "breakthrough" looks like in the real world.

All of these real-life heroes understood the Slight Edge. None of them were hypnotized by the allure of the "big break." If they had been, they would never had continued taking the actions they took—and what would the world look like today?

One Small Step...

Our cultural mythology, the philosophy our society subscribes to as a group, worships the breakthrough even when we don't realize that's what we're doing.

"One small step for a man ... "—nonsense! That wasn't one small step—the guy was on the moon! That was one gigantic step for man, a genuine breakthrough.

The small step was when some guy—someone you and I never heard of—first started tinkering with design ideas for how a rocket ship might withstand the intense conditions of space flight. There were thousands, hundreds of thousands, millions of "one small steps" for years and years beforehand that all went into that epic 1969 leap of Neil Armstrong's that was televised throughout the world (and is still played over and over in our culture as one of the most deeply ingrained news bites of history).

But we don't celebrate any of those real "small steps." We don't even know what they are, or who made them.

The myth of our culture is the giant step, the larger-than life leap, the heroic effort. "Faster than a speeding bullet, able to ... " Wait, how does that go again? Is it, "able to take small, insignificant, incremental steps, consistently, over time?" No, it's "able to leap tall buildings in a single bound!" I mean, what kind of Superman would take tiny steps?

The kind who wins. Like Edison and his light bulb.

There's a popular expression these days, "Luck is preparedness meeting opportunity." It's a nifty little saying, and it's close, but in my experience, it isn't quite accurate. Luck is preparedness—period! Preparedness through doing those simple, little, constructive, positive actions, over and over. **Luck is preparedness that eventually creates opportunity!**

That's the truth of big breaks, lucky breaks and breakthroughs: they do happen—just not out of thin air.

Have you ever suddenly understood something in a "flash of recognition"? Have you ever known of someone who became an "overnight success"? Here is a secret: both that "sudden flash" and that "overnight success" were the final, breakthrough results of a lengthy process of edge upon edge upon edge. You may completely and absolutely trust in the truth that it is always the little things, done consistently over time, which bring about the "breakthroughs" that you see.

No success is immediate. Nor is any failure instantaneous. They are both products of the Slight Edge.

The truth of quantum leaps is that they are not larger than life: they're submicroscopic. The actual term "quantum leap" comes from particle physics, where it does not refer to a huge, epic jump. It refers to the fact that energy, after a period of time, will suddenly appear at another level, without our having been able to observe how it got there.

It is an exact description of how the water hyacinth moves from day twenty-nine to day thirty. An exact description of how the frog's certain death by drowning was suddenly transformed into salvation by butter.

A real-life quantum leap is not Superman leaping a tall building. A real quantum leap is Edison perfecting the electric light bulb—and transforming the world with it.

The "Magic Bullet"

Every single January in every gym in America, hundreds of thousands of people start over in a process that they will soon quit—only because they haven't set themselves up with the right expectation. They aren't looking for incremental progress; they're looking for results they can feel. They're looking for a breakthrough. They never had a chance.

Easy to do, easy not to do ... and in that tiny, seemingly insignificant little choice *not to do*, so many people needlessly live out lives of quiet desperation.

Believing in the "big break" is worse than simply being futile. It's actually dangerous, because it can keep you from taking the actions you need to take to

One Quality Story at a Time

My good friend Mark Victor Hansen and Jack Canfield, co-authors of the blockbuster *Chicken Soup for the Soul* series of books, understood that long-term success is built not only on being prepared, but by offering a quality product that people will continue to buy for years and years to come.

I remember sitting with Hansen when he and Canfield had a vision for a book concept that had never been done before. As speakers, they were known for their motivational stories and quotes they would weave into their speeches. Fans loved their stories so much they inquired if they could put these stories and quotes into a book. Instead of using their own stories, they reached out to fans and others to submit stories of people doing extraordinary things. All they had to do was carefully edit and compile them into topics that people would want to read. Once they had one title down, their plan would be to do other titles based on the same format.

I have to admit, I wasn't too sure that was a very good idea. In fact, I told Hansen he had a 50/50 chance of success. I didn't know if people would want to read a collection of stories written by everyday people. But they had a clear vision of what they wanted to do, how they were going to do it and how they were going to get there. It wouldn't be a slap-it-together-and-shove-it-out-the-door kind of project. They knew it would take time to get the right stories, and a lot of work went into evaluating each and every story they put in—101 to be exact in their first book. They also knew the name of the book would be key, for they wanted the stories to have a healing effect, much like the chicken soup Canfield's mother would give him as a child. The name stuck.

When it was released in 1993, the media didn't pay much attention or have much use for it. But word-of-mouth spread like wildfire and many people were buying several copies at a time to give to family and friends.

By September of 1994 *Chicken Soup for the Soul* was on every best-seller list in the U.S. and Canada. Over the next ten years, Chicken Soup for the Soul branded merchandise reached over $2 billion in retail sales. As of this printing, over 112 million books—not to mention CD and DVD collections and many other products—have been sold in over 200 titles and 40 languages.

Hansen and Canfield weren't looking for a quantum leap to success. They knew that one quality story at a time would eventually get them to where they wanted to be.

create the results you want. It can even be lethal. Think of the poor frog that gave up and let himself drown because he couldn't see a breakthrough on the horizon. He was wrong, of course: there are miracles, even in the life of a frog. It's just that the breakthrough didn't come down out of the clouds; it came at the end of a series of consistent, determined, compounding-interest foot-paddlings.

What's the greatest gift you can give to an inner-city kid? An understanding of the Slight Edge. Because that's not the answer he's getting from the world around him. He believes that the only way out of his world of poverty, violence, oppression and fear is to become a sports superstar—because that's what we tell him. That's the quantum leap answer. The truth, of course, is that very, very few individuals will have the talent to break out of that world by becoming sports superstars. And deep down, every one of these kids knows that, or soon finds out ... so they give up. Why bother? And they become victims of the Quantum Leap Myth. Can you imagine if every first grader was required to start reading 10 pages of a good book a day? How would their finances, their health, their relationships change as adults?

Slight Edge for Teens: Making a Difference

A few years ago we partnered with the SUCCESS Foundation to write *SUCCESS for Teens: Real Teens Talk About Living the Slight Edge*. It's a wonderful book that skillfully illustrates the importance to young kids of clarifying their goals, while practicing the small efforts necessary for success, and accepting responsibility for one's own destiny. Organized in an easy-to-read format and sprinkled with engaging exercises, action steps and stories from real teens, *SUCCESS for Teens* helps teens embrace eight principles that will allow them to shape the futures that they want.

For more information, log on to www.successfoundation.org. The SUCCESS Foundation, along with its partnering organizations Big Brothers Big Sisters, Boys & Girls Clubs, Network for Teaching Entrepreneurship, Just Say Yes, America's Promise Alliance and Optimist International, are committed to distributing worldwide more than 10 million *SUCCESS for Teens* books and audios to instill the Slight Edge philosophy in today's youth.

Crisis of Poor Health

Over the last several decades, it's been amazing to me how many people I've been close to have persisted in making fun of my dietary choices, exercise habits and personal development goals. The "insignificant" little things I've been doing every day for years have always struck them as funny, because they couldn't see the point. They couldn't see the results coming further on down the path.

Today I see these friends and ache for them: many now have failing health, are languishing in poor financial conditions and seem to have lost their hopes for the future. What they have a hard time seeing is that my good health isn't an accident, and their poor health isn't a stroke of bad luck. We've all gotten to where we are today the exact same way: the Slight Edge. They are victims of the Quantum Leap Myth.

Our society is sliding rapidly into an ever-increasing economic crisis of poor health including an epidemic of adult onset diabetes, heart disease, obesity and a score of other chronic illnesses that have steadily fed a monstrously overgrown health care system, tax system and social security system—and there isn't a single "cause" anywhere in sight. As I'm writing this, several of our most widely used over-the-counter drugs have suddenly been found to make things worse.

There is no mystery for those who know how to recognize the Slight Edge at work. Our entire health crisis is nothing but one set of little decisions, made daily and compounded daily, winning out over another set of little decisions, made daily and compounded daily.

We look for the cure, the breakthrough, the magic pill—the medical-scientific quantum leap miracle our press has dubbed the "magic bullet." But the solution already exists. It always did. Is it magic? Yes—the same magic that caused the problem: the power of daily actions, compounded over time. The magic of the Slight Edge.

There's a great line in the movie *Bruce Almighty*, when God (played by Morgan Freeman) is leaving the all-too-human Jim Carrey character to solve things on his own (and refusing to be a *deus ex machina*). He says, **"You want a miracle? Be the miracle."** Once you absorb the Slight Edge way of being, you'll stop looking for that quantum leap—and start building it. **You too can become the miracle.**

The Winning Edge

The Slight Edge is the process every winner has used to succeed since the dawn of time. Winning is *always* a matter of the Slight Edge.

One of the most highly anticipated events at the Summer Olympics is men's swimming. Going into the 2008 Beijing Games there was a lot of hype surrounding Michael Phelps, who would be gunning for Mark Spitz's 36-year-old record of seven gold medals. The first seven medals came rather easily, but his eighth medal was one for the ages: the 100 meter Butterfly. When he came down the final stretch, it looked like he was going to fall just inches short. After touching the wall, the world was stunned when the clock showed Michael had edged out Milorad Cavic by 1/100 of a second. Yes, that's a very slight edge. But it's all he needed to secure a record eighth gold medal, perhaps becoming the greatest Olympic athlete ever. What if he had lost by 1/100 of a second, would we be calling him the greatest Olympic athlete ever? Probably not.

Do you know what makes the difference between a .300-hitting baseball star with a multimillion-dollar contract and a .260-plus player making only an average salary? Less than one additional hit per week over the course of the season. And you know what makes the difference between getting that hit and striking out? About one quarter-inch up or down the bat.

No golf fan will ever forget the Master's tournament where Phil Mickelson was left with a twenty-foot putt on the eighteenth hole of the final round. Miss it, even by one inch, and he would head into a playoff with the number two player in the world, Ernie Els. Make it, and he would finally silence the critics and win his first major. The putt rolled in and Mickelson had his green jacket.

Over the course of the tournament's four days, Mickelson shot a 279, six strokes better than his competitor. The difference? One and one half strokes per day better. The Slight Edge.

And it's not just in sports. It's in everything.

In 1998, a book called *The Millionaire Next Door*, by Thomas J. Stanley and William D. Danko, became a runaway best-seller. What so amazed readers was the fact the people profiled in the book were incredibly ordinary, everyday sorts of folks, with normal and even mediocre-level jobs, who had created extraordinary wealth by a truly remarkable, unexpected, amazing strategy. It consisted of—you guessed it—doing little, mundane, ordinary, insignificant, everyday things with their money.

If you had followed any of those people around for the twenty or thirty or forty years during which they were amassing their financial empires, I promise you, it would not have been breathtakingly exciting—no more exciting than it would be to follow an Olympic athlete in training every day from his 3:30 A.M. wake-up call to his exhausted collapse into bed at night.

We love rags-to-riches stories and underdog-becomes-hero stories, and we use them to motivate people because they are so exciting and dramatic ... aren't they?

Actually, no. The truth is, they're not exciting at all—when they're really happening. They only seem dramatic in the retelling. But the reality is that the rags-to-riches success story person has gotten to where he is by making mundane, quiet, little Slight Edge decisions and repeating simple disciplines, day in and day out.

It's not exciting to read about; it's not exciting to make a movie about. It's not even exciting to do. But believe me, it sure is exciting when you finally get to experience the results.

No matter in what arena in life or work or play—the difference between winning and losing, the gap that separates success and failure, is so slight, so subtle, most never see it.

Superman may leap tall buildings at a single bound. Here on earth, we win through the Slight Edge.

KEY POINTS OF CHAPTER 5

We look for the cure, the breakthrough, the magic pill—the medical-scientific quantum leap miracle our press has dubbed the "magic bullet." But the solution already exists. It always did. Is it magic? Yes—the same magic that caused the problem: the power of daily actions, compounded over time. The magic of the Slight Edge.

I grew up as the seventh of eight kids. We did not have a lot of money. Nobody in my family had a college degree but I had big dreams for my future! How would I make them become a reality without the advantages of the wealthy and successful showing me the way? How could I start with nothing and truly live the American Dream? A close relative was always pursuing the next Gold Mine, investing in the "just discovered" oil well, the "next big thing." I thought, "Is this the way to pursue my dreams?"

I discovered the Slight Edge principles and started channeling the burning desire I had for success into the correct daily habits and I knew that over time, I would build momentum that would help me to reach my goals. I knew that by consistently working towards my goals with a positive attitude, I would see my dreams become a reality! Boy, was I right! I've had the privilege to travel the world, raise a great family, do things I've never dreamed of—all because of these principles! Unfortunately, my close relative still is pursuing the "next big thing."

> —*Dennis Windsor*
> *Author, Financially Free!*

After reading *The Slight Edge* I realized how I ended up where I was in life. I was like a ship without a rudder, a wandering generality. I have always known I wanted to be successful, however, I never realized that it was not that big chance or huge deal that was going to do it. I finally understood it was the day to day events that I did or did not decide to do that made the true difference in my life. As I sat and looked at my life I finally got the picture. From that day forward I started to apply the Slight Edge to everything I was doing from business to relationships. Although it was hard at first, once I got used to doing the little things everyday it made all the difference in the world. I now have a wonderful woman in my life, a thriving business and time to reflect on what is most important to me.

> —*Adam Russell, Miami FL*
> *Principal / CEO Global Resource Broker LLC*

CHAPTER 6

The 7 Slight Edge Principles

By now you have learned what the Slight Edge is all about—how it can work for you or against you. You have also read about the importance of doing the little things every day that don't seem like a big deal but are a big deal—seemingly insignificant tasks done daily that add up to success.

You have also learned how I have implemented the Slight Edge philosophy into my life and how it has been the core foundation for my success. And by now, you have perused through some of the stories of *The Slight Edge* readers—people from all walks of life whose lives have changed by adhering to the Slight Edge philosophy.

I am overwhelmed and humbled each and every time I read about how ordinary people are now living extraordinary lives just by adding a few daily disciplines to their daily regimen.

As I pore over the thousands of notes and letters we have received over the years, I began to see a pattern of certain principles these people followed that are a part of the Slight Edge philosophy—principles that I have taught in some form over the years, but have never put down on paper until now.

I was able to isolate seven specific and actionable principles that you can apply right now and use as a guidepost as you head into the next part of the book. Before you can master the Slight Edge in your own life you need a game plan to guide you along the way.

No. 1: Show Up

> *Hope begins in the dark, the stubborn hope that if you just show up and try to do the right thing, the dawn will come. You wait and watch and work: you don't give up.*

— Anne Lamott

Woody Allen, the famous playwright, once said that 80 percent of success is showing up. I am one that subscribes to this philosophy wholeheartedly. You have already won half the battle if you will commit in showing up every day. The rest is left up to skill, knowledge, drive and execution.

The story of Jorge Diaz epitomizes the importance of showing up every day no matter the circumstances. Today he is a professional boxer who in November 2010 defended his Featherweight crown in Atlantic City and has a record of 15-0 as of this printing. Not bad for a kid who grew up in one of the toughest neighborhoods in New Jersey.

After reading *The Slight Edge* in 2006, he said the book changed his philosophy and approach to the sport of boxing. Here is a short segment of his story:

> *I have been boxing since I was 11. I am from a tough neighborhood and had very young parents who were struggling financially, so we didn't have money for a boxing trainer to spend one-on-one time with me, but I applied the Slight Edge principles and showed up to the gym to practice every single day—nothing could stop me from showing up.*
>
> *For years I would lose at finals or walk away with a bronze. More often than not I lost in the finals of national events. Even when I was upset from losing, I firmly believed in the Slight Edge principles and the compounding of my efforts. Ten years later I am now starting to see the fruits of my labor and am currently the Featherweight champion with a record of 15-0.*
>
> *Now that I am a little older and wiser I firmly believe at a greater level in all the philosophies of* The Slight Edge. *I have learned how to use my past as a tool to help make my ride to the future a little easier. I firmly believe that if I keep my simple daily routine consistent, with nothing fancy, just keep refining my craft and keep swimming in the bucket of milk, I know that it will turn into butter.*

Wow! Jorge had every excuse not to show up to the gym every day, but he did it anyway because he knew that by doing the little things every day it would eventually give him the strength, discipline and smarts to bring him the Featherweight championship. Congratulations Jorge on your success!

I had the distinct pleasure of teaching this principle to my daughter Amber when she achieved her life-long goal of becoming a Gator at the University of Florida. For those who know me there is no bigger fan of this school. I had spent my daughter's early years giving her not so subtle hints as to where she should go when the time came to choose a college. I guess my prodding worked!

It was at her freshman orientation when I was able to share with Amber the importance of showing up. We, along with thousands of other incoming freshmen and their parents, were sitting in the audience when the dean of students announced from the podium that they had 6,700 incoming freshmen that year. Of that group, the average GPA average was a 4.0. The SAT scores were in the top 10 percent of the nation. Intimidating words, to say the least. I wasn't sure if he was trying to motivate or scare them. Amber, I was afraid, was feeling the latter.

This would her first true competition since high school, where she also averaged a 4.0 GPA. But she knew that her natural talents that got her to the top of her high school class may not be enough to give her an upper hand in college.

To ease her anxiety we went out to dinner and the first question out of her mouth before we ever sat down was "Dad, I'm going up against the best of the best. What am I going to do to get an edge on my classmates?" Calmly but surely, I said to her, "It's going to be so easy to beat these students." Amber rolled her eyes and was a little worried what she was getting herself into.

What I shared with her were some simple philosophies that would lay the foundation for her college career. I said, "First off, you can beat half of these kids simply by showing up." Sounds too easy, right? I could tell Amber was still a little confused by the simplicity of my statement. But I wasn't done. I told her, "If you will also go to every single class, even when those around you will pressure you to stay home, you will beat half these students by outlasting them." I could tell things were starting to click a little in her mind. Amber was already used to going to school every day in high school. This was something she could do. She did it for four years in high school. I could tell by the look on her face she was starting to believe me. But the lesson had just begun.

No. 2: Be Consistent

In baseball, my theory is to strive for consistency, not to worry about the numbers. If you dwell on statistics you get shortsighted; if you aim for consistency, the numbers will be there at the end.

— Tom Seaver

Showing up is important, but its natural companion consistency is what makes it a powerful duo. Showing up consistently is where the magic happens. I told Amber she not only needed to show up every day for school but it had to be coupled with at least two hours of study per day. Again, this was something Amber already knew how to do from high school that had led her to a 4.0 GPA. From my own experience I know how easy it is to get caught up in the vicious cycle of cramming for tests. My advice to her was to leave that to the others. This lesson also came with a disclaimer.

These things, *though easy to do*, were also very *easy not to do*. She would be challenged by roommates and other friends to skip class for other campus activities that I know are all part of the college experience. I could tell she was starting to get what I was saying, but could it be that simple just to show up every day for class and study for two hours a day?

The first sign of success came three weeks later when Amber called and said, "Dad, remember that class I have with 400 students in it? Well, there are only 80 people who come now." So what could have happened in three weeks? Amber said they hadn't had a test yet so no one could have flunked out. In less than three weeks, 75 percent of her class was gone. I told her to just keep showing up and to study for two hours a day.

Four years later, right on time, Amber graduated at the very top of her business class just by doing those two simple things—easy. principles that if applied daily can yield fabulous results.

Amber wasn't any better or smarter than the other kids. They were the cream of the crop, top-notch students. But Amber had one distinct advantage the others didn't: she had a philosophy that drove her to stay on course even when everyone else was doing the opposite. She showed up consistently and succeeded because she had a simple philosophy that she applied every day, rain or shine.

Consistency Yields Results

I am a big sports fan and sports always make wonderful metaphors for life. The lessons learned from sports are many and are used frequently when I speak to large audiences. One of them is the importance of consistency. To be a great football team, not only do you have to practice every day, but practicing includes running the same plays over and over again until everyone gets them right, so all that is left is the execution.

Head baseball coach and *The Slight Edge* reader Russell Stockton of Houston knows firsthand how constant repetition pays off for his team. In his 20 years as a head baseball coach, mostly at smaller colleges, he never had the luxury of landing a "blue chip" recruit for his team. To equal the playing field a few years ago he instilled the Slight Edge principles into his coaching philosophy. And it has produced amazing results, earning him a conference title and a trip to the NCAA Regional tournament for the first time in 10 years.

Stockton has also been very successful in getting his team to buy into mastering the simple fundamentals of the game. In a letter he sent us, he tells of one pitcher, who wasn't expected to break into the starting rotation at the beginning of the season, but ended up being one of the most valuable players on his team come playoff time. Here is his story.

> *I was a new assistant coach at the university and was assigned to the pitchers. The head coach gave me the rundown on all the guys and told me who to spend the most time with. This one player, we will call Tom, he told me not to spend much time with him, as he was a non-factor. However, this player bought into the Slight Edge concept that I taught him and he did the drills religiously. By the end of the year, because he applied the Slight Edge principles and had improved his game so much, he was drafted in the third round and signed for a little less than $500,000. He should be in the big leagues next year.*

Stockton has also been very successful in getting his team to buy into mastering the simple fundamentals of the game. The best example Stockton uses in how he implements the Slight Edge philosophy is with his hitters.

> *I tell my hitters, when practice is over, if they choose to, go to the batting cage and hit two buckets of balls, approximately 100 swings, it will only take about 20 minutes (easy to do). However, most leave and go home (also easy to do). But if they take 100 extra swings five days a week they will have 500 extra swings by the end of the week. I tell them they probably will not be much better. But don't stop, do that all four weeks of the month. So by the end of the first month they should have 2,000 extra swings.*
>
> *You might start seeing a positive change. But don't stop; if you do this for all 10 months of the school year, by the time we hit the playoffs you should have 20,000 extra swings. But if you can take at least five teammates with you to the batting cages, then our team will be getting 100,000 extra swings. The year we won the conference title I had six to eight hitters who bought into this idea.*

There are some who won't be as dedicated as the baseball players led by Coach Stockton in doing the little things every day. Some people when they get the tiniest amount of freedom fall off the wagon and stop doing everything they were taught to do. Why does this happen? Simply because they are now in an environment where they find themselves with no structure—no one telling them what to do. The principles of showing up consistently give people the structure they will need in their lives in portions they can handle.

No. 3: Have a Good Attitude

Attitude is a little thing that makes a big difference.
— Winston Churchill

Not only do you need to show up consistently, you need to do it with a good attitude. Why is attitude so important? According to author and leadership icon John C. Maxwell, attitude makes all the difference in the world. I got the chance to interview John recently on the topic of attitude and he told me the following:

> When all things are equal, attitude will set you apart from anything else. When you're going for a job, it's the difference maker. If a girl has a choice between two handsome men where one has a great attitude and the other one has a lousy attitude, nine times out of 10 she's going to pick the man with the best attitude. It's a difference maker for coaches who have two athletes who are of similar skill level and are looking for who to play. Attitude really is the difference maker.

Having a good attitude has proven to be a key in longevity of life. I was watching CNN one night and a well-known doctor was talking about a report he had just released where he studied the 25 longest living civilizations on earth, where people lived well past the age of 100.

He went through the process of finding out the common threads these successful civilizations have in common. Keep in mind these civilizations were not connected by race, geography, DNA or genetics. In his findings the number one characteristic—far greater than number two—that determined whether you live over 100 years of age, is a positive outlook on life.

Attitude my friends, attitude. Many would think it would be their diet or their genetic code that determines one's health. That obviously is true, but the difference maker, as John C. Maxwell alluded to earlier, is our attitude—our positive outlook on life—the key factor for us living long and productive lives.

And with as much traveling and speaking as I do, I've developed this uncanny ability to spot givers and the takers when it comes to attitude. Givers are those people who brighten the room with their positive vibe and excitement for life. Takers are those who immediately seem to dim the room with their lack of excitement and depressing outlook on life.

I can feel a "dimmer" coming toward me from far away. There could be 50 people in the room and I could spot the one who is sucking the life out of the room. I just run from these kinds of people. I'm looking for people with an infectious positive attitude, who bring energy, vitality and who brighten the room, not dim the room with their nagging and negativity.

Beware of the Cuckoos

It's hard to have a good attitude with all that is going on in society. Negativity can show up at your doorstep every single day, seven days a week, with or without your permission. We are constantly bombarded by negative messages from the media and other sources that can impact the way we look at life.

Why do you think publishers put magazines and newspapers where they do in grocery and convenience stores? Because that's where they have the best chance of selling you their fish wrap, to put it bluntly. But I will tell you right now, there's not one thing in those magazines that you need to know—not one thing that is going to help you lead a better life. Those magazines are "cuckoo."

Cuckoos are not limited to magazines and other news media outlets. They are people we work and associate with on a daily basis. Now let me tell you something right up front. I have worked with a lot of different people from all walks of life in my career. Many have been hard workers, committed-to-a-cause kind of people who have an incredible ability to get things done. On the flipside, I have also worked with those who are just plain cuckoo. They are professionals in the art of distraction, who take people's attention away from the task at hand. They will drive you crazy if you let them.

You have people just like this in your office. They congregate at the water cooler and dish out the latest gossip on who's doing what, complain about how much they hate their job, and even make fun of people who are trying to improve the workplace morale by being beacons of positivity. Again, there are people who brighten the room, and there are the cuckoos at the water cooler, folks who dim the room with their negativity.

When I was in my 20s and building my solar company in Albuquerque, New Mexico, there was a lady named Carol Cooke, an industry icon who knew everything and anything about the solar business. She had some sage advice for me about these "dimmers." She said, "Jeffrey, here is how I see it. There is one born every minute, and the sad thing is most of them live."

What Carol gave me was a philosophy, an attitude, and she basically said, you're not going to change how some people are. Some people are just cuckoo, and there is just no getting around it. But here is what you need to ask yourself. Am I going to let these people frame how I feel about myself? Because I'll tell you what folks, the "cuckoos" are not going away. And they are going to do everything in their power to make you join them in their craziness. Don't listen to them.

How to Inoculate Yourself from the Cuckoos

One of my all-time favorite books is *Think and Grow Rich*, the timeless classic written by Napoleon Hill. He was commissioned to write the book by Andrew Carnegie, the wealthy steel magnate and one of the most famous philanthropists of all time. Hill traveled the globe to interview the world's 500 most important people of his era. His task was to break down the characteristics they have most in common and write a book about it.

One of the traits they had in common was they believed you needed to create a mastermind group of like-minded people who see things the way you do in order to inoculate yourself from the cuckoos (the original text doesn't say "cuckoos," but I'm pretty sure Hill would have agreed with the name).

Now what does this finding tell us? Remember, these were some of the smartest people in the world at the time yet they built a system to inoculate themselves from the masses of negativity. My opinion is if you do the opposite of what the majority does, nine times out of ten you're going to be right. That's why Arthur Schopenhauer, the great German philosopher and businessman, hundreds of years ago said "Every truth passes through three stages before it is recognized. In the first it is ridiculed, in the second it is opposed, in the third it is regarded as self-evident." To put it simply, just because you encounter opposition from "dimmers" and are ridiculed for stepping out of your comfort zone by putting out positive ideas and solutions, you cannot allow these people to frame what you know to be true.

It takes a lot of guts, faith, perseverance and a healthy dose of positive attitude to go through the public ridicule and opposition of people telling you your ideas are worthless.

Embrace the Funk

It's hard to stay positive with so much negativity out there in the world today. And no matter how you try to inoculate yourself from the "cuckoos," no one is safe from their grasp, me included. Let me tell you a story that will help illustrate what I mean.

I was speaking in Palm Springs to a crowd of about 2,500 people. At the end of my speech I wanted them to be able to ask any question about the presentation I just gave. For the next three hours we had a Q&A session, and halfway through it a woman from the audience took the microphone; I remember she had a strong presence about her. She said to me, "Jeff, you obviously take care of yourself, you are very successful ..." Then she got to a part that I will never forget.

She proceeded to say, "What are people like us supposed to do? A lot of us are looking to get what you have. What is the secret to getting through the tough times?" This is a question I had never received before and I was a little stumped at first. Just then I received a little inspiration from somewhere and proceeded to tell her that there are days when I wake up and I'm in what I call "the funk," where life feels heavy, depressing and I just don't want to get out of bed because I just don't feel right.

The first thing I do when I'm feeling this way is I take inventory of my blessings. I have people who love me, I have great relationships, I'm healthy, I'm financially independent, etc. But it still doesn't go away immediately; in fact, sometimes it takes several hours or days to get out of the funk.

Now I don't have much to complain about, but the funk still gets me. I don't think it matters how "successful" you are in life, the funk is still going to get you at times. It comes for everyone—it doesn't discriminate.

I told that woman that, number one, she is normal. Everyone gets the funk. But here is what I have learned. I finally came to a realization one day (this is what saved me) that there is no way I can understand love, if I haven't felt hurt. I can't know good without knowing what's bad. I can't feel happy and content without feeling the funk. Life is ebb and flow.

So when bad things are happening to you, you need to "embrace the funk" with the principles you have learned in this book. When something is hard or difficult and adversity is at your front door, embrace it, because it will refine you like a refiner's fire and make you stronger. You can't know happiness unless you feel sadness. If you embrace it as part of the process, I tell you it can be life altering. This has helped so many people get unstuck.

Life is going to get you down and the funk is going to get you. Embrace it and fight through it and know you are not alone. You are no different than anyone out there. Without knowing you and what your strengths and weaknesses are, I *feel* like I know you, because I've met hundreds of people who are just like you, who have applied these Slight Edge principles to take baby steps out of the funk, and it has made a huge difference in their lives.

The Happiness Movement

So much of projecting a positive attitude begins with having a positive and happy outlook on life. The tough economy we're going through surely has changed the definition of happiness for many people. Things that made us happy a few years ago may not make us happy today. And the search for what makes people happy and its effect on those around us has spawned a new movement the likes of which I have never seen before. Do a Google search on "happiness books" and you'll be amazed at how many best-selling books deal with the topic of happiness.

In the *Happiness Advantage*, author Shawn Achor spent 10 years studying the topic of happiness and his research resulted in some very interesting observations.

In his book he breaks down the conventional wisdom that says if we work hard and have success, then—and only then—we will be happy. We say to ourselves "If I could only get that promotion or lose 10 pounds then I will truly be happy. Success first, happiness second. Achor says his research—as well as other studies—prove that it's actually the other way around: that happiness is the precursor to success, not merely the result.

Achor states in his book the following:

> *If we are positive our brains are more alert and engaged, free to create, which eventually leads to more productivity ...happiness and optimism actually fuel performance and achievement—giving us the competitive edge that I call the Happiness Advantage.*
>
> *Waiting to be happy limits our brain's potential for success, whereas cultivating positive brains makes us more motivated, efficient, resilient, creative and productive, which drives performance upward. This discovery has been confirmed by thousands of scientific studies and in my own work and research on 1,600 Harvard students and dozens of Fortune 500 companies worldwide.*

Delivering Happiness Is Big Business

No one knows that happiness precedes success better than Tony Hsieh, the CEO of Zappos.com. Tony's journey includes making Zappos.com one of the hottest and most beloved online retailers. He grew the company from almost no sales in 1999 to over $1 billion in gross sales, annually. That got the attention of Amazon.com, who purchased the company for $1.2 billion in 2009. Hsieh's success comes down to one philosophy: delivering happiness—happy employees and happy customers equals success.

Tony understood that delivering outstanding customer service as an online retailer can be tough. Since customers can't touch and feel what they are buying, they need to go the extra mile in eliminating any and all customer fears of buying online by offering free shipping both ways. If something doesn't fit, send it back for free. Zappos looks at these extra costs as marketing expenses, a minor tradeoff in their eyes for a customer who raves about their shopping experience. In essence, they are creating what they call a WOW experience, which their customers remember for a long time and usually tell their friends and family about.

Zappos.com employees are just as passionate about delivering happiness through outstanding customer service as their fearless leader. This is due to the culture that Hsieh and his executive team have developed with their employees. They are not just order takers, but invested partners committed to delivering the best customer service in the industry.

In his book *Delivering Happiness*, Hsieh describes their core philosophy:

> *At Zappos.com, we decided a long time ago that we wanted our brand to be about the very best customer service and the very best customer experience. We believe that customer service shouldn't be just a department, it should be the entire company ... What's the best way to build a brand? In a word: culture. Our belief is that if you have the culture right, most of the other stuff—like great customer service, or building a great long-term brand, or passionate employees and customers—will happen naturally on its own.*

It is refreshing to see scientific studies that tout a positive attitude as a precursor to success and to see big companies integrating it into their culture. Hard work will always be an ingredient for success, but when mixed with a happy disposition and good attitude, not only will you begin to experience the fruits of success, but you will also attract others to help you along the way.

No. 4: Be Committed for a Long Period of Time

It takes a long time to grow an old friend.
— John Leonard

Let's summarize where we are so far. First, we need to show up, be consistent and have a good attitude. The fourth Slight Edge principle is to practice these principles for a long period of time. Just as a farmer has to wait a full season to reap his harvest, you must do the same. In my opinion, this is the hardest principle for our microwave and fast-food culture to deal with because we want instant results now, not in 120 days or a year from now!

Showing up consistently with a good attitude for a short period of time isn't going to cut it. You've got to show up consistently with the good attitude, being patient and persistent for a *long* time to create lasting change.

There is a great book called *Outliers* by Malcolm Gladwell that illustrates this point perfectly. There is a chapter in the book where he brings to light his research into some of the most important industries—software and manufacturing giants, educators, the military—and how many hours go into making a product good enough to where they are ready to sell it on the open market. What they found was it took about 10,000 hours before they really got good at it. That's 40 hours a week, times five years.

Like these industry giants, you've got to show up with the good attitude and you've got to put in your 10,000 hours or more before you come close to mastering anything, let alone golf, which will take a bit longer … like your lifetime!

That's the reason why I wrote *The Slight Edge*, to show people there is no shortcut to success. No matter what you are trying to accomplish, you need to ask yourself, *Am I willing to put in 10,000 hours or more to get what I want?*

Give Yourself Time

I've been around the personal-development world for a long time. While I was CEO of The People's Network, we were the largest producers of personal-development content in the United States. I was blessed to be sitting in that position during the most exciting time in personal-development history.

The one problem I noticed within the personal-development arena is those who buy into the "Quantum Leap" theory as discussed in Chapter 5. In order for authors to sell books, they need to convince you that their program is going to change your life in a certain amount of time. Most people are looking for a quick fix and aren't interested in learning the truth: that success doesn't come overnight or even in few weeks or months. It takes a lot of time and a lot of hard work.

Take the story of *The Slight Edge* reader Tray Honeycutt from Victorville, California. He struggled with his weight for many years and he just couldn't seem to make any changes. He was looking for the quantum leap answer. Two days after finishing the book he decided to put the Slight Edge to the test. Over the course of 40 weeks he lost 60 pounds, and got in such good shape that he became a personal trainer and started teaching the principles of *The Slight Edge* to his clients.

You see, he didn't have to starve himself on some fad diet or exercise for hours like they do on *The Biggest Loser*. It really came down to a few disciplines compounded over time that made the difference for Tray.

Once successful people find something that works, they repeat that action over and over again with a good attitude over a long period of time until they are successful. Eventually the compound effect will kick in, just like in Tray's case. And that's all this book is about. Trying to get people to slow down and realize that you are not going to feel the results of your actions immediately.

In fact by the time you feel the results, you have already done most of the work. The problem is that most people are not willing to show up consistently and stay in the game long enough with a good attitude for a long period of time because they have the wrong philosophy.

The problem is that most of these "90-day programs to a better you" don't give you enough time to build up a belief level in yourself that you can continue past the 90-day time period. By committing to things that are manageable to implement every day you greatly increase your chances of success. As discussed in earlier chapters, I tell people to simply read 10 pages of a good book a day. Not just for 90 days, but for 250 days. (I'm giving you 115 days off because I'm a nice guy. If you show up every day and read 10 pages, that'll be 2,500 pages by the end of the year. *That's about 10 books.*)

And if you are reading the right stuff, it's not only going to help form your philosophy, but it's also going to shift your attitude, is it not? You see, what most people do is they read a book and then they don't go back and read it again. You'll learn so much more the second time around. Give yourself more time and you will be impressed by how much you retain by taking your time to get it right and to learn from your mistakes.

No. 5: Have Faith and a Burning Desire

> *There is one quality which one must possess to win, and that is definiteness of purpose, the knowledge of what one wants, and a **burning** desire to possess it.*
> — Napoleon Hill

Of the 500 most successful people who Hill interviewed in *Think and Grow Rich*, the number one commonality among them was faith along with a burning desire. Desire is what gets you up early and keeps you up late. It's what keeps you motivated to press forward when adversity hits.

There are going to be all types of obstacles placed in front of you during your lifetime. And you can determine the size of a person by the size of the problem that keeps them down. **Successful people look at a problem and see opportunity.**

You have to change your philosophy about problems because they are always going to be there. They are a part of everyday life and they are not going away. You have to have a burning desire to get through, just like *The Slight Edge* reader Aaron Grove:

> *For as long as I can remember I wanted more in life; however, I grew up poor, from humble beginnings. That is where my burning desire started. I'll never forget the day that the philosophy of the Slight Edge was introduced to me. Most vividly I can recall reading this book every morning and starting right then to implement small activities, daily, assured this would be the way over time—to physical fitness, eating right, building and maintaining relationships, building my business and finances, spiritual alignment, etc. I knew consistently showing up with a good attitude for a long period of time would get me to where I wanted to be. And then one day, Presto! Results were visible!*

Aaron had a burning desire to make the changes in his life. By implementing those small activities into his daily regimen, he got the results he needed. Just like Aaron, you have to show up consistently with a good attitude over a long period of time with a solid desire to change the trajectory of your life.

No. 6: Be Willing to Pay the Price

> *Leaders aren't born, they are made. And they are made just like anything else, through hard work. And that's the price we'll have to pay to achieve that goal, or any goal.*
>
> —Vince Lombardi

Anything worth having is worth working and paying a price for. That's the price of entry. And If you're not willing to pay a price for whatever it is you want, the price of neglect is far worse than the price of commitment. In Chapter 10 we will get into this topic a little more in detail, but I would like to preface this principle here first.

Years ago it hit me that if I didn't choose to do something to become successful, I was going to become unsuccessful for the rest of my life. Think about that. If you don't figure out something to be successful at, you have to be unsuccessful at it for the rest of your life.

In other words, the price of neglect is pretty brutal. The price of committing to something, showing up consistently with a good attitude over a long period of time while having faith and a burning desire and being willing to pay the price is far easier than the true price of neglect. **But there is a price that you're going to have to pay.**

I'd like to introduce you to Pablo Felix, who I think is one of the best examples I can find of someone who was willing to pay the price for what he wanted. Pablo had one slight disadvantage. He has been deaf since birth. Slight Edge principles have been instrumental in both his business and personal life. Here is his story:

> *Unfortunately, my parents did not realize that I was deaf until the age of 6, when I started preschool. I began learning American Sign Language upon entering school and spent many years trying to overcome my language delay.*
>
> *Because my family never learned sign language in order to communicate, I was always left out of family decisions. When a serious family situation came up, I was never even told what had happened. Time and time again I was given little or no information necessary to make sense of the world because it took too long or was too difficult to attempt communication.*
>
> *As a result of being left out of so many experiences, I developed a sense of not belonging even to my own family. Like most people my age, after college I got married and started a family of my own. I dreamed of getting a good job and climbing the corporate ladder. I quickly found that corporate America held no place for a deaf person. I was regularly passed over for promotions and treated like a second-class citizen. I was denied access to the very information needed to be an effective manager.*
>
> *For many years, I carried lingering resentments from the past. Even though my wife and children could hear, I found it difficult to overcome the disconnect I felt with mainstream society.*
>
> *I decided to start my own business in order to control my future. I decided I needed to learn from other successful people so I interacted with people who could hear, more than ever before in my life.*
>
> *After being told that reading was a critical aspect of my new endeavor, I began my journey of personal development. I realized that my life was not on the path necessary for success. I was on a downward slope along the path of blame, until I discovered the Slight Edge. I was able to change the negative compounded effects of years of unhappiness to a life of responsibility. My life became full of hope, excitement and joy.*
>
> *I was able to finally release my resentments; I began setting goals for both my personal and professional life. I was able to attain many of professional goals and even outperform many of the people in my field. I now have had the pleasure of helping many more deaf people reach success.*

I teach them the importance of positive daily focus. We track our desires, goals, personal development, and accomplishments in notebooks, titled, "What Do You Want?" This simple daily activity compounded over time has kept us on the positive upward path to success. I strive daily to become a better leader, father and husband by applying Slight Edge principles to my life.

Instead of whining about it and letting his employer continue to brand him as a problem rather than a solution, Pablo made the necessary changes in his life to find his calling by helping members of his deaf community find value and purpose.

No. 7: Practice Slight Edge Integrity

> *Integrity is not a conditional word. It doesn't blow in the wind or change with the weather.*
> — John D. MacDonald

There are many definitions of integrity, but the one most applicable to the Slight Edge is what you do when no one is watching, and that is what I call

Slight Edge integrity. It is also doing the thing you said you were going to do long after the mood you said it in has left you.

Most kids when they leave the comfort and structure of high school and home life are rudderless—like fish out of water. They are not used to the freedom and responsibility placed on them once they are out on their own making decisions for themselves. Many fail to plan and prioritize their time and end up making poor decisions. Their integrity in doing the little things every day has been compromised by the lure of freedom and being on your own.

My daughter Amber didn't have to have integrity when she was young because we were there to help her make those choices. But when she left the nest and went to school 1,500 miles away, this responsibility fell to her. She would have to put into action the philosophies we taught her growing up. We were no longer there to help her or look over her shoulder to make sure she was making correct decisions. The integrity clock for Amber was already in motion. Would she do those daily disciplines when no one was watching? Would she show up consistently and study two hours a day like she was taught? Thankfully she did and she was rewarded for it. She was willing to do the little things—those daily tasks that seem insignificant to most people.

Kobe Knows Slight Edge Integrity

As I've stated throughout the book, I'm a big sports fan because so much of life is woven throughout the tapestry of sports. Those in the Hall of Fame are individuals who didn't have to be prodded or told what to do to become successful. It was ingrained in them. Kobe Bryant in many sportswriters' opinions has taken over the mantle as the best player in the game. LeBron James might have another opinion, but the facts are truly in Kobe's corner. Why?

Sports Illustrated polled 190 NBA players and asked if they could have anyone in the NBA on their team for one game, who they would want to take the last shot with the game on the line. It wasn't even close:

Kobe Bryant, *Lakers* G.....76%
Chauncey Billups, *Nuggets* G.....3%
LeBron James, *Cavaliers* F.....3%
Paul Pierce, *Celtics* F.....3%
Dwyane Wade, *Heat* G.....2%

What does this have to do with integrity? Not much, but it teaches a more important lesson. The poll is just the end result of Kobe Bryant's insatiable desire to become the greatest basketball player in the world. No one had to tell him as a young man he needed to spend hours outside of practice honing his craft. He did it on his own when no one was watching. For Kobe Bryant, taking the last shot when the game is on the line is second nature because he has practiced it so many times on the blacktop when no one was watching—because he knew that is what he needed to do to succeed. The only difference is he gets paid an insane amount of money to do it now.

Slight Edge Business Integrity

The same can be said about those who venture into starting their own companies. Why is the failure rate so high for startups? Most everyone knows that lack of capital is by far the biggest reason companies don't make it past two years. But there is also an integrity component that is the cause for so many business failures.

When you own a business, there is no one telling you that you need to be at work or shouting in your ear to make sales calls. No one is there to make sure you are on top of your vendors and your books are up to date. This is up to you to do now. And many business owners just don't have the Slight Edge integrity it takes to remain above water. They become intoxicated by the freedom of being their own boss and fail to maintain the kind of structure to become successful.

Yet there are many startups that do put into practice the Slight Edge integrity it takes to make it. Jeremy T. was a highly ambitious 24-year-old gym owner, and for him, success couldn't come fast enough. It wasn't until he read *The Slight Edge* that he realized that success would need to be slow and steady and consistent over time. He needed to take inventory of what it would take to become successful and apply those steps consistently with or without anyone watching to make sure he did them. Two years later Jeremy's business quadrupled:

> *I have opened two additional gyms, an online media company and we're on track to quadruple our revenue once again. Since reading* The Slight Edge *I am no longer looking into the unknown, but instead looking to the present possibilities that are ingrained in my daily habits. The book gave me a paradigm shift. I have faith that my daily habits will lead to success or failure, the choice is mine. Pay attention to your daily habits and it will pay off.*

The Slight Edge gave Jeremy a structure, a foundation, a daily philosophy he could implement that has brought him success. And you too can use Slight Edge integrity to improve your health, your relationships, your personal development, etc. You name it, the sky's the limit. It just takes discipline, hard work and a desire to change.

Are You Ready to Do the Little Things When Nobody Is Watching?

There is a great quote that says "If you add a little to a little and do this often, soon the little will become great." Whether it was at school, corporate America or starting my own business, that quote has been the formula I have used my entire life to gain the Slight Edge.

Once we published *The Slight Edge*, it has taken on a life of its own. The stories I have shared with you in this chapter and throughout the book are a testament that the philosophy works. Jorge became a featherweight champion, my daughter Amber graduated at the top of her business class, Coach Stockton's baseball players were drafted into the Major Leagues, Pablo overcame his lack of hearing to become a valuable member of his community, and Jeremy has taken his gym to unprecedented heights.

These are everyday people, who by implementing Slight Edge principles into their lives have done amazing things. Successful people do the little things that seem to make no difference at all when they are doing them. Doing them over, over and over again, consistently and persistently, with a good attitude over a long period of time, is what the Slight Edge is all about.

Just as my daughter asked me how she could separate herself from the pack, you have the chance to do the same. And in doing so, not only will you change yourself but you may also change the people around you.

KEY POINTS OF CHAPTER 6

Over the years I have isolated seven actionable principles that you can apply right now into life, every day. Show up consistently with a good attitude over a long period of time. Have faith and a burning desire, be willing to pay the price and have slight edge integrity and discipline to do those things even when no one is looking.

By the age of 30 on paper I was worth a million dollars. I owned land, businesses, oil wells, I was even the President of the Chamber of Commerce, an upstanding citizen of the town— life was good. In the next decade at the ripe age of 40 all that had changed. I found myself newly divorced, bankrupt with five children to support. My self-esteem was in the toilet. A chance encounter with an old acquaintance changed everything. He had an opening at his company that he offered me and just as important he recommended some great books and resources I should start reading to get my psyche back on the right track.

When I started this new job we were discussing my salary. I told him, "I will work for free and you can tell me what I am worth." I was a tele-marketer making cold calls all day. My nights were spent on the floor of the office space I worked from as I couldn't afford my own place. Each day I was the first to work and the last to leave. I would stay on the phone making hundreds of calls with every response imaginable, mostly not so favorable. I knew that I had within me the ability to turn my life around once again. For that to happen it would require me each and every day to practice the principles of the Slight Edge. It would require that I set goals and do the daily disciplines that eventually, not miraculously, would lead me to the vision I was holding for my life. I mastered the mundane, day in and day out. About six weeks into the job I had ZERO sales but persevered knowing that I was developing my skills as a telemarketer and that it would pay off.

That day came when I was informed that one of the largest insurance companies purchased over 150 tickets for their agents and would be purchasing the same for another event we were promoting. At that time it was the largest single sale ever made at this very well-established company. I was eventually given the title of 'Vice President' and was made a 50 percent partner of the company. All of this transpired because I showed up consistently over a long period of time with a good attitude. I had a burning desire and faith and was willing to pay the price. And I was willing to do all this even when no one was watching. I am now living out my dreams and making a positive difference sharing the profound but simple principles of the Slight Edge.

—*Steve Fleming, Santa Fe, New Mexico*

CHAPTER 7

Two Life Paths

Two roads diverged in a yellow wood
And sorry I could not travel both
And be one traveler, long I stood
And looked down one as far as I could
To where it bent in the undergrowth.

Then took the other as just as fair
And having perhaps the better claim
Because it was grassy and wanted wear
Though as for that, the passing there
Had worn them really about the same.

And both that morning equally lay
In leaves no step had trodden black
Oh, I kept the first for another day!
Yet, knowing how way leads onto way
I doubted if I should ever come back.

I shall be telling this with a sigh
Somewhere ages and ages hence
Two roads diverged in a wood
And I took the one less traveled by
And that has made all the difference.

— Robert Frost, *The Road Not Taken*

There was a time when the people of the world were convinced the sun revolved around the Earth. A few visionaries stubbornly refused to accept what was obvious to everyone else, and because Copernicus, Galileo and a handful of others risked their lives to choose the road less traveled, the rest of the world eventually caught on to what is now obvious to everyone in the twenty-first century: the Earth revolves around the sun.

What's more, in the last hundred years, we've discovered that even space is curved (though that one's still a little hard for most people to wrap their minds around).

The truth is, *everything* is curved. There is no true straight line; everything is changing—including your life.

You are on a journey, your life path. That path is a curve.

You're curving either upward or downward.

It may seem to you that today was much like yesterday. It wasn't. It was different. Every day is. Appearances can be deceiving—and almost always are. There may be times when things seem to be on a steady, even keel. This is an illusion: in life, there is no such thing as staying in the same place. There are no straight lines; everything curves. If you're not increasing, you're decreasing.

Above and Below the Slight Edge

Let's take a look at what the Slight Edge actually looks like by going back to the wealthy man's lesson. If you make a graph of the penny doubled every day for a month, it will look something like this:

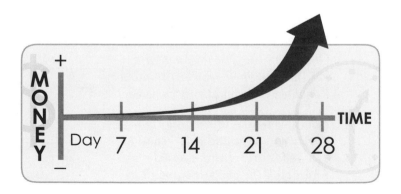

This is not only a picture of compound interest; it's also a picture of how the Slight Edge looks when it's working *for* you.

Now, let's get a sense of what the Slight Edge looks like and feels like when it's working *against* you instead. It's simple: just put a mirror up to the first illustration. This graph shows you that when it's not working in your favor, the Slight Edge can be a very sharp and unforgiving edge indeed!

If you understand and live by the law of compound interest, your life will look like the upper half of this graph. If you don't understand and live by the law of compound interest, your life will look like the lower half of this graph.

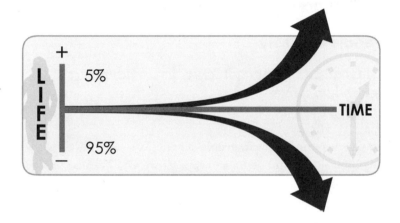

Wherever you may be in your own life, understanding the Slight Edge will give you the tools to start fresh—right now!—and place yourself firmly on the upper curve.

The upper curve is the formula for success: a few simple disciplines, repeated every day. The lower curve is the formula for failure: a few simple errors in judgment, repeated every day.

The upper curve represents that one person out of twenty, the five percent who are successful and happy at the end of their lives. The lower curve represents the other nineteen, the ninety-five percent who reach their "golden years" angry and bitter, and have no idea or concept of how they got there or why. Life, it seems to them, is unfair, and that's just how it is. But you and I know that's not the case. It's not a matter of being fair or unfair: it's pure geometry, the geometry of time.

Most people hold time as their enemy; they seek to avoid the passage of time and strive to have results now. That's a choice based on a philosophy. Successful people understand that time is their friend. In every choice I make, every course of action I take, I always have time in mind: time is my ally. That, too, is a choice based on a philosophy.

Time will be your friend or your enemy; it will promote you or expose you. It depends purely upon which side of this curve you decide to ride. It's entirely up to you.

If you're doing the simple disciplines, time will promote you. **If you're doing the few simple errors in judgment, time will expose you—no matter how well you appear to be doing right now. Time is the great equalizer.**

Why People Don't Fly

> *If God had meant man to fly, he would have given him wings.*
>
> — Bishop Milton Wright

Have you ever wondered why people can't fly? We have a phrase we use when something difficult, painful or tragic happens; we say, "Whoa: that's heavy." And indeed, it is. Life is heavy. The predominant force on Earth is gravity, and gravity is always pulling you down.

Just ask Bishop Milton Wright, the founder of Huntingdon College in Huntingdon, Indiana, who is reputed to have pointed out the self-evident truth in the quote above during a sermon he delivered in 1890.

Some people, though, just can't seem to accept self-evident truths. Like two of Bishop Wright's sons, who thirteen years later built and flew the first successful, man-powered, heavier-than-air flying machine. Their names were Wilbur and Orville.

Social science research says that as a child, you heard the word "No" about 40,000 times by the age of five—before you even started first grade. How many times had you heard the word "Yes"? About 5,000. That's eight times as many no's as yes's. Eight times the force holding you down, compared to the force lifting you up. Eight times the gravity against your desire to soar.

Don't do that! Don't say that to your grandmother! Don't slouch! Don't touch that, it's hot! Don't talk to strangers! Don't cross the street! No ... No ... No ...

Mind you, most of these no's are well intended; like the police force motto, their purpose is only to protect and serve. So I'm not criticizing the no's. But where are the yes's?

Author Jerry Wilson, in his landmark book *Word-of-Mouth Marketing*, based his revolutionary "exceptional customer service" strategy on a statistic he'd found: the average customer will tell three people about a positive experience with a business or product, but will talk about a negative experience to *thirty-three* people! Eleven bad experiences to one positive; eleven reasons an idea won't work to one reason it will.

I mentioned earlier that only about one person out of twenty will ever achieve his or her goals and dreams in life. Regardless of what realm of life or work or play we're talking about, we'll see an average success rate of not more than five percent. Why is that?

Forty thousand no's to five thousand yes's. Thirty-three negatives to every three positives. Is it any wonder that ninety-five percent of us are failing? Is it any wonder most people don't fly?

If you are one of those rare and special five-percenters who decides to ignore gravity and take to the sky—one of those rare birds, like Orville or Wilbur, who chooses to break free of the downward pull of life and rise to a higher quality of life, accomplishment and success, to be a pioneer and risk discomfort and ridicule for the sake of your dreams—well, I've got good news and bad news.

The good news is, you're already exceptionally well oriented toward success.

The bad news is, all those ninety-five others are going to be yanking on you, sitting on you, naysaying and doomsaying on you, and doing their level best to pull you back down. Why? Because if you succeed, it reinforces that they are not where they want to be.

They know instinctively that there are only two ways to make their building the highest building in town: build an even bigger one—or tear down all the others. Since the odds are against most people building the big one, and since it takes just too darn long to start seeing any results, and since they are not at all aware of the Slight Edge, they're taking the path of least resistance, and going into the demolition business.

You can use the Slight Edge to break free of the downward pull of life and become the best you can possibly be. Or, the Slight Edge will pull you down, keep you down, and eventually take you out of your life. It's up to you.

For things to change, *you've* got to change. For things to get better, *you've* got to get better. It's easy to do. But it's easy not to do, too.

Blame and Responsibility

*A man can fail many times, but he isn't a
failure until he begins to blame somebody else.*

— John Burroughs

If you want to measure where you are, if you want to know whether you're on the success curve or on the failure curve, or if you want to assess anyone else and determine which curve they're on, here's how. There is one attitude, one state of mind, which overwhelmingly predominates either side of the curve.

The predominant state of mind displayed by those people on the failure curve is *blame*. The predominant state of mind displayed by those people on the success curve is *responsibility*.

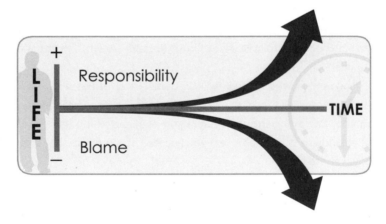

People on the success curve live a life of responsibility. They take full responsibility for who they are, where they are, and everything that happens to them.

Taking responsibility liberates you; in fact, it is perhaps the single most liberating thing there is. Even when it hurts, even when it doesn't seem fair. When you don't take responsibility, when you blame others, circumstances, fate or chance, you give away your power. When you take and retain full responsibility—even when others are wrong or the situation is genuinely unfair— you keep your life's reins in your own hands.

Negative and difficult things happen to all of us; most of them are mostly or completely out of our control. It's how we react, how we view those circumstances and conditions, that makes the difference between success and failure—and that is completely within our control.

The five-percenters who dwell on the upper curve know there are no excuses; they understand and accept the fact that nobody can do it to them, and nobody can do it for them. They live by the axiom, "If it's going to be, it's up to me." They set their own standards—and their standards are high. They realize that their only limitations are self-imposed. They understand that it is not what happens to them that's important, but how they respond to what happens that makes the difference between their failure and success.

They are aware of the Slight Edge and they understand how it operates in their lives.

People on the failure curve are masters of blame; they blame everyone and everything—the economy, the government, the oil crisis, the weather, their neighbors, the rich, the poor, the young, the old, their kids, their parents, their boss, their co-workers, their employees. Life itself.

The inhabitants of the lower curve are life's victims, the great mass of "done-to's." The only way these folks can really make much sense of out life is to conclude, "Life is a bitch—and then you die."

I knew a man whose self-declared philosophy was, "Life is an unpleasant practical joke which occurs somewhere between birth and death." On which side of the curve do you think he was living? Where was he headed? Can you imagine what results that thought, "Life is an unpleasant practical joke," would create when magnified by the water-hyacinth-like force of time?

You know the expression, "Be careful what you wish for—you just might get it"? It's not even a question of what you wish for: be careful what you think. Because what you *think*, multiplied by action plus time, will create what you get.

People on the failure curve are oblivious to the Slight Edge—or, if they are aware of it, they take a position of opposition, as if their lives were dedicated to proving that it isn't real or doesn't really work.

> *Responsibility is declaring oneself as cause in the matter. It is a context from which to live one's life.*
>
> *Responsibility is not a burden, fault, praise, blame, credit, shame or guilt. All these include judgments and evaluations of good and bad, right and wrong, or better and worse. They are not responsibility ...*

Responsibility starts with the willingness to deal with a situation from and with the point of view, whether at the moment realized or not, that you are the source of what you are, what you do and what you have.

It is not "right," or even "true," to declare oneself as "cause" in the matter. It's just empowering. By standing for yourself as cause, "what happens" shifts from "happening to you" to "just happening" and, ultimately, to "happening as a result of your being cause in the matter.

—Werner Erhard

Don't Complain About What You Allow

The people on the upper half of the Slight Edge curve are the cause of what happens in their lives. They view all the forces that brought them to this point—God, parents, teachers, childhood, circumstances, you name it—with gratitude and appreciation and without blame. And they view themselves as the cause for what comes next in their life.

Are you your own cause?

The people on the upper curve take full responsibility for all the choices they make in their lives and in their work. Do you? It's easy to do ... and just as easy not to do. And if you don't take full responsibility for your thoughts and actions and circumstances right now, will that kill you today? No ... *but!*

But that simple error in judgment compounded over time will absolutely, positively destroy you.

Successful people do what unsuccessful people are not willing to do: they take full responsibility for how the Slight Edge is working in their lives. **Unsuccessful people blame the Slight Edge for their lives not working. Successful people know that they cannot afford that luxury.**

Past and Future

Try this experiment: Take a comfortable, seated position and look down at the floor; then, without changing position, take the next five minutes to think about your life. Anything and everything, whatever that means to you, just think about your life.

Go ahead and do that now ...

"My recovery is a symbol of persistence, courage and the Slight Edge."

by **Tracy Broughton**, *2011 Ms. America®*

As Ms. America® 2011, there is a lot of glitz and glamour that come along with the title, but behind the glamour, what is really important is one's real foundation which should be built around character. I want to share my story with you in hopes that in some way it inspires you, and that you know that all of your dreams are attainable by having faith and determination and taking daily action to get there.

I was born a fighter, three months pre-mature, doctors said I was not going to make it but I had other plans. In elementary school, my mother was diagnosed with stage four cancer and given six to eight months to live. I still remember the day that my mother told me to not worry about her cancer and that she would see me graduate high school. Unfortunately, in junior high there were many challenges at home that caused us to move eight times, in and out of the state, within several years. I even lived on my own for a period of time, luckily with financial help, because of the uncertain environment in the household. While helping take care of my three siblings, my mother and working, I persevered through traumatic times in my life by doing the little things, in each area of my life, that didn't seem to make any difference at the time I did them. I knew that if I persevered I would arrive at the doorstep of my dreams eventually. I went on to be a scholar athlete, played varsity sports, set school records, and took on many leadership roles at school, including Senior Class Vice President.

Two months after graduating high school, about six years longer than they gave her to live, my mother passed away. I went on to pursue my modeling career. I channeled my energy and efforts into building my career. I worked tirelessly, doing the things every day that were easy to do, easy not to do, and was featured in magazines, calendars, catalogs, TV shows, videos, billboards, fashion shows, commercials and beauty pageants.

I believe that the perseverance that it takes to succeed in modeling and acting is the same thing that helped me with my recuperation after not one, but two car accidents. In October of 1991 and December of 1996 I was in major car accidents and sustained severe injuries that caused me to be admitted in to the Intensive Care Unit and the hospital for months. In 1996 I was diagnosed Hemiplegic, I was paralyzed on the left side of my body, and I was confined to a wheelchair.

My philosophies and faith are constants in my life, and they have helped me through recovery and have continued to influence my life in a positive direction. Through occupational and physical therapy, my rehab included working on my speech, learning to tie my shoes, preparing food, transferring, bathing, and being able to accomplish everyday needs on my own. Through years of therapy, at the hospital, with doctors, at PT, in the gym, and at home, sometimes one to three times a day, I had to stay consistent with a positive attitude. There were years of little or no improvement or progress, yet I continued to believe and work towards walking. The hard work seemed to make no difference at all, but it was internal motivations that fueled my actions. I looked past my current circumstances, and focused on the end result that I was trying to achieve. And defied what many thought, that "I would never walk again." I am now walking! There were no extrinsic rewards for the subtle stages of progress over the last fourteen plus years, these rewards only came when others were able to see me stand up and then later walk. My continued recovery is a symbol of persistence, courage and the Slight Edge.

I went on to make public appearances, win contests and I eventually resumed my entertainment career. After running three offices in corporate America, I eventually opened two of my own businesses: a florist and a legal insurance business. I am a loving single mother of 11-year-old identical twin sons. I was in my wheelchair when I had my twins and raised them for many years from the wheel chair. I had many reasons to blame others or circumstances throughout my life, but I chose to take responsibility for my future no matter what circumstances were presented to me.

By doing the things that are easy to do, yet make no difference in the act of doing them over a long period of time, I was able to, as a single mother, become a successful business owner, servant leader, speaker and friend, as well as go from wheel-chair bound to Ms. America® 2011!

A true testimony to the Slight Edge!

To inquire about Tracy Broughton's speaking availability and or to learn more about Tracy Broughton, visit www.tracybroughton.com

The Ms. America® Pageant is for women 26 years of age and up who are single, divorced or married. To learn more about the pageant go to: www.MsAmericaPageant.com.

Now, clear your mind, walk around a minute, then come back and do the second half: Take the same comfortable, seated position, only tilt your head up so you're looking at the ceiling. Spend the next five minutes thinking about your life. Anything and everything, whatever that means to you, just think about your life.

Go ahead and do that now ...

I don't know what results you had, but here's what most people find: when looking down, it's pretty hard not to start thinking about the past. When gazing upward, it's pretty hard not to start thinking about the future.

I can promise you, that morning in the Phoenix airport, every single person I saw rushing around was looking either straight ahead, or down!

People on the failure curve tend to focus on their past—and it pulls them down. People on the success curve focus on their future—and it pulls them up.

People on the success curve don't ignore the past, but they use it as a tool, one of many with which they build their futures. People who live on the failure curve use the past as a weapon with which they bludgeon themselves and the people around them. Regrets, recriminations, remorse and retribution.

It seems most people live with one foot in the past, saying "Only if things had been different, I would be successful." And the other foot in the future, saying "When this or that happens I will be happy/

successful." And they completely ignore the present, which is all we really have. It's only the decisions that you make in the moment that are Slight Edge decisions.

A friend of mine says that people make two lists about their spouses and carry these lists around in their heads. The long list is a list of "what's wrong," and they consult that list every day. The short list is a list of "what's right." That's the list they read for the eulogy.

People on the success curve don't wait until the funeral. They burn the long list and spend every day reading from the short list. They make themselves experts in "what's right," and let go of "what's wrong." They never hold a grudge—not because it's morally wrong (although they may agree with that reason, too), but because it gets in the way. It slows them down. They're too busy moving toward the future to be staring into the rearview mirror.

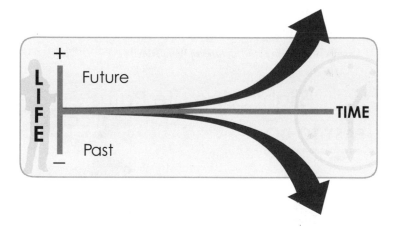

One of the quickest and most direct routes to getting yourself up and onto the success curve is to get out of the past. Review the past, but only for the purpose of making a better plan. Review it, understand and take responsibility for the errors you've made, and use it as a tool to do differently in the future. And don't spend a great deal time doing even that!—the future is a far better tool than the past.

The future is your most powerful tool and your best friend. Devote some serious, focused time and effort into designing a crystal-clear picture of where you're going. In the second part of this book, we'll take a look at specific ways to help you do exactly that. For now, I'll just say this: when you do have a clear picture of the future and consciously put time every day into letting yourself be drawn forward by that future, it will pull you through whatever friction and static you encounter in the present—and whatever tugging and clutching you may feel from the past.

One last thing about past and future—and I *have* saved the best for last. **You can't change the past. You can change the future. Would you rather be influenced by something you can't change, or by something you can?**

Where Are You Headed?

> *Would you tell me please, which way I ought to go from here?" "That depends a good deal on where you want to go," said the Cat. "I don't much care where—" said Alice. "Then it doesn't matter which way you go," said the Cat. "—so long as I get somewhere," Alice added as an explanation. "Oh, you're sure to do that," said the Cat, "if you only walk long enough.*

— Lewis Carroll, *Alice's Adventures in Wonderland*

Slight Edge Life Paths

5% SUCCESS
Progressive realization of a worthy idea

EASY TO DO
Simple disciplines made consistently over time

- Responsibility/Discipline
- Value Driven

What's uncomfortable early becomes comfortable later

PHILOSOPHY → ATTITUDE – ACTIONS – RESULTS – **LIFESTYLE**

What's comfortable early becomes uncomfortable later

- Blame/Neglect
- Entitled

FINANCES
HEALTH
BUSINESS
PERSONAL DEVELOPMENT
RELATIONSHIPS

EASY NOT TO DO
Simple errors in judgement made over time

95% FAILURE
Lasts a lifetime

On which side of the Slight Edge curve are you standing right now? Which way are you headed? Are you one of the five-percenters, one of those individuals living on the success curve and going up—or are you among the great majority, the ninety-five percenters on the failure curve and sliding down?

Not sure? Perhaps, in the middle, you say? Sorry, there is no middle. You are either going up or going down. The early part of both curves are fairly flat, so it can certainly look like you're moving along on a nice, even keel, heading neither up nor down. But appearances can be deceiving. (And usually are.) In a constantly and rapidly changing world like ours, you simply cannot remain the same as you were yesterday. You are in motion—you have no choice in that.

But in which direction? You have total choice in that.

You are either improving or diminishing in personal and professional value. Your relationships are growing deeper and richer, or growing more stale and distant. You are learning more and more about the truths of life, or slipping deeper and deeper into denial about the truths of life. You are building your long-term security and financial freedom, or dismantling it. And your health is building day by day ... or ebbing slowly away.

There is no treading water in life, no running in place, because everything is in motion. If you're not improving, enriching, building, unfolding, if you're not adding assets to your personal and professional value every day—then you're headed down the curve.

So, let's take an honest look at your life. Where are you right now?

Let's take an honest look at your health.

Are you building it every day? The way you eat, the way you exercise, the kind of schedule you keep, the ways in which you take care of yourself—are all these building a greater feeling of health and vibrancy every day? Or does it feel like you're making more and more withdrawals from your life-energy bank account, and the balance is steadily decreasing?

Is your health on the success curve or failure curve?

Let's take an honest look at your personal development.

Are you learning more about yourself, about the world around you, and about how life works every day? Are you learning new skills and sharpening old ones? Are you becoming a more capable person, one more interesting to know and valuable to be around? Or is your character being gradually etched with the age-lines of disappointment, disillusionment, boredom and bitterness?

Is your personal development on the success curve or the failure curve?

Let's take an honest look at your relationships.

Is the number of friends in your life, people with whom you stay in touch, with whom you share meaningful exchanges and mutually enriching experiences, growing larger every year? If you are married, and you were to describe your marriage as a plant, would it be a plant that is growing taller, riper, fuller and richer with each passing year? What about your family—children, parents, brothers, sisters and others? Are they growing deeper and richer or more distant and shallower?

Are your relationships on the success curve or the failure curve?

Let's take an honest look at your finances.

Are you building assets and putting money into a long-term plan that will create true financial freedom? Is your net worth growing larger each year?

Are you living within your means and investing a portion of your income into a program that will build equity for you over the years, growing dollar by dollar and picking up momentum through the power of compounding interest so that, like a snowball rolling down a wintry hill, it will have gathered tremendous financial mass in the years when you need it most?

Or are you living on credit, on borrowed money as well as borrowed time, running your coffers empty and storing up debt instead of equity, digging yourself deeper and deeper into a hole that grows only harder to escape?

Are your finances on the success curve or the failure curve?

Let's take an honest look at your life itself.

What kind of impact is your life having on the world around you? How is the world different as a result of your being here? After you leave this world, what will you leave behind as a legacy and how will people remember you? When you add together your career and all your professional accomplishments, your relationships and all your personal accomplishments, your sense of connection with nature, humanity and God, how would you describe the overall value or meaning of your life? And is that sense growing stronger, deeper, richer, more powerful every day, month and year?

Is your life on the success curve or the failure curve?

Be honest about all of this. Do as Shakespeare's Polonius tells his son Laertes to do:

> *This above all, to thine own self be true; and it must follow, as the night the day, thou canst not then be false to any man.*

—William Shakespeare, *Hamlet*, Act 1, Scene 3

If you don't tell the truth about where you really are in your life—right now—then you're cheating yourself out of an extraordinary opportunity. **Because right now, this very minute, can be the time you look back on as the moment your life changed for the better—forever!**

Life is not a practice session; there's no dress rehearsal. This is it. This is for real. So, play straight and true with yourself. Take a look at your life and tell the truth about where you really are at.

Do this exercise with me right now. Take a pencil (not a pen—remember, everything changes) and put a check in the UP or DOWN box next to each area of your life as listed below. Which way are you going?

	UP	DOWN
Your health	_____	_____
Your personal development	_____	_____
Your relationships	_____	_____
Your finances	_____	_____
Your life itself	_____	_____

Where are you? Which side of the line do you fall on in each area of your life?

If you have more "down" checks than "up," I have two things to say: the first is thank you for being honest! And the second is, don't worry, you're not alone. Remember, gravity has been pulling you down since day one. Remember that you've heard eight no's for every yes, and eleven negative comments for every positive one! And those no's and negatives are compounding with the force of the water hyacinth, threatening to cover the surface of your mind with a suffocating weed that blots out all possibility of sunlight reaching the life that's wanting to thrive there. The one or two "no's" didn't kill you—but those 40,000 can sure do some serious damage to your sense of possibility.

That's the Slight Edge working against you.

The Good News

Now, here's the good news: where you are right now is poised in the present, with the past stretching behind you and the future lying ahead. You cannot change the past. You can absolutely change the future.

Are you heading up, or heading down? Right at this moment, at this exact juncture in your life, you

can answer the question either way. At any moment in your life, you can choose to change which side of that curve you're on.

The good news is the wealthy man's third gift: you have a choice.

Where you've been heading is not necessarily where you will be heading after you turn this page, or put down this book, or wake up tomorrow morning. The past does not equal the future. In fact, you cannot look in both directions at once. You can look down, or you can look up; you can look back, or you can look forward; you can look in the rearview mirror, or at the highway ahead.

Step onto the upper curve, the path of success, and you will put any area of life—your health, your finances, your relationships, your family life, your career, your spiritual health, your sense of accomplishment and fulfillment and purpose—on track within a few years.

If you don't step onto the upper curve? Failing is something that will take the rest of your life. Failure, unchecked by a choice to change, is a life-long condition.

What matters now is your awareness of how the Slight Edge operates in your life and your understanding that you have what you need right now to change that. All the information you need is already out there—and, right here. You're already doing the actions. All you need to do is choose to have to them serve and empower you—and *keep on choosing*.

In my line of work, I talk a lot about success in financial terms. But genuine success is a far greater issue than purely financial health. A genuinely successful life means your health, your family relationships, your career, your spirituality, your sense of fulfillment, your legacy and the impact you have on the world. It's all these things and more. And the best thing about genuine success is that it spreads! **Success in any one of these areas begins to affect all the others, too. Improve your health and you improve your relationships; work on your personal development and you have an impact on your career. Everything affects everything else.**

If you are having a hard time making progress in one area—say in business— take action to make a small positive change in an unrelated area. Start taking a walk around the block, organize that junk drawer that has been haunting you. Feeling successful in one area will provide you with renewed confidence and energy to continue on your journey of attaining that other big goal.

The Ripple Effect

When you create positive improvements in your life, a positive ripple effect is created all around you. You become a better relative, friend, business associate, and community member, which in turns creates a bigger positive impact on society than simply the change created in you. When you reach out and positively affect another person through your interactions and words, you create a slight change in that person, who is then more likely to reach out and positively affect someone else. Simply put, one touches another, who touches another, who touches another. You are constantly creating a ripple effect by the way you affect your environment. It can either be a positive ripple or a negative ripple. The choice is always yours.

Take action now to start casting your positive ripples. Do you have every resource you'll need to accomplish everything you want in life ... right now? No. Can you put your hands on all those resources right now? No.

But can you make a choice—and come up with one penny?

That's all it takes to start.

KEY POINTS FOR CHAPTER 7

The truth is, everything is curved. There is no true straight line; everything is changing—including your life. You are on a journey, your life path. That path is a curve. You're curving either upward or downward.

Wherever you may be in your own life, understanding the Slight Edge gives you the tools to start fresh—right now!—and place yourself firmly on the upper curve.

How to Handle Blame and Responsibility

Before reading this book, I tended to lead a life of blame. I never accepted any responsibility, it was never my fault, always someone else's, or something that prevented me from succeeding. After reading the book, I realized I had a decision to make: continue on my path of failure, or change. Sometimes it seems like it's too late in life to change things. I realize now it is NEVER too late. You have to start somewhere! It's up to the individual to dig deep, look at things from the past, and strive to be better in the future with just a few simple changes.

—Charleigh Vigil, Dekalb, IL

I was an alcoholic and this was taking over every ounce of goodness and skillfulness I once had. Fortunately, destiny had a better plan for me. I made the decision to fight my enemy. I enrolled myself in a rational sobriety outpatient facility. At the same time, another positive occurrence happened: I was introduced to *The Slight Edge*. The simple principles described in the book were an absolute revelation for me. By understanding how I had let my worst enemy work the magic of the Slight Edge to my disadvantage, I was able to take the appropriate baby steps necessary to change the curve of my life! Today, I am free and happy. I wake up in the morning energized, I am aware of which steps are necessary to achieve my goals and I walk along a path which leads me, a day at a time, to fulfillment.

—Michele Tremblay-Suepke, Tacoma, WA

PART TWO
Mastering Your Life

CHAPTER 8

Mastering the Slight Edge

It resists definition yet can be instantly recognized. It comes in many variations, yet follows certain unchanging laws. It brings rich rewards, yet it is not really a goal or a destination but rather a process, or journey. We call this journey mastery and tend to assume that it requires a special ticket available only to those born with exceptional abilities. But mastery is not reserved for the supertalented or even for those who are fortunate enough to have gotten an early start. It's available to anyone who is willing to get on the path and stay on it— regardless of age, sex or experience.

The trouble is that we have few, if any, maps to guide us on the journey or even to show us how to find the path. The modern world, in fact, can be viewed as a prodigious conspiracy against mastery. We're continually bombarded with promises of immediate gratification, instant success, and fast, temporary relief, all of which lead in exactly the wrong direction ...

— George Leonard, *Mastery*

Mastery is not some vaulted, lofty place that only the elite few ever land. The pursuit of any aim, goal or dream—personal, professional, spiritual, in any area—is a Slight Edge journey of continuous improvement, learning and refinement. But **mastery is not an exalted state that lies at the end of the path; it is a state of mind that lies at the**

very beginning. According to George Leonard, author of *Education* and *Ecstasy and The Way of Aikido*, mastery is the act of setting your foot on the path.

As a fifth *dan* black belt in Aikido and an award-winning writer on education, fitness and personal development, Leonard has more than a passing acquaintance with mastery, and what this master has to say about the subject is remarkably liberating.

There are no shortcuts, he says, no special tickets needed, and none available even if you wanted one. You don't need to be born with exceptional abilities to enter into mastery, nor is it reserved for the supertalented. You don't even need to have gotten an early start.

The upward journey of success on the Slight Edge curve is available to anyone who is willing to get on the path and stay on it. **But it's only by being immersed in the process, the day-by-day progression, that you will come to know the road.** That's how you will acquire and refine the skills and awareness you'll need to master the Slight Edge and, therefore, master your success and your life.

All that's required is taking the first step.

Baby Steps

When you were a tiny child, you made your way around your world on your hands and knees, crawling. Everyone around you was walking, and one day you got it into your little head that maybe you could give that a try. And once you had that thought, you had to give it a try. It was simply the next frontier; there was no way you weren't going to master it.

So, step by step—literally!—you worked on developing the skills you needed to walk.

You grabbed onto something above you and pulled yourself upright. You stood up, holding on to a playpen or chair or some big stuffed animal. You were wobbly and unsure. You let go, either on purpose or by accident, and it didn't matter which, because the result was the same—*Crash!* You fell down. And then, either right away, or later that day, or the next day (and it didn't matter when), you tried it again. And then you tried it again, and again ... until eventually, you stood up all by yourself—no hands.

Then you took a step—and in that step, according to George Leonard, you assumed the mantle of mastery ... even if external appearances didn't entirely confirm your new status. (Remember, appearances can be deceiving—and almost always are.)

So here you are, just completing your very first step. Now, you know that the big people you've been watching go around taking one step after another. You've watched them do it: right foot, left foot, right foot, left ... so you try. You complete that first, tentative, epic-making step and get ready to swing into the next one—and then, *Crash!*

Try again. And again. And again. After days of side-stepping around the coffee table, awkwardly bringing one little foot out from behind the other while you hold onto Mom's or Dad's fingers, you eventually take your first sequence of two steps ... then three, and four, and ... all alone ... all by yourself ... and to the encouraging cheers and applause of your proud family—baby steps ... one at a time ... *and you're walking!*

In the process of learning to walk, did you spend more time falling down or standing up? If you were anything like most babies, you failed (fell) far more than you succeeded (walked). It didn't matter: you were on the path of mastery.

Did you ever have the thought of quitting? Did you ever say to yourself, *You know, it looks like maybe I'm just not cut out for walking ... oh well. I guess I'll just have to crawl for the rest of my life—which really isn't all that bad, when you stop and think about it. I'm sure I'll get used to it ...* ? Of course not. You were on the path of mastery. You were already a master—now it was only a matter of your walking skills catching up.

Constantly falling down was really uncomfortable—it hurt!—and you probably looked pretty silly lying there on the floor like a beetle on its back ... but you kept at it anyway. Why? Because successful people do what unsuccessful people are not willing to do—and *all babies are successful.* All babies are masters; we're designed that way. All babies instinctively understand the Slight Edge. We only let go of our natural pull towards success, our mastery, over the course of those 40,000 no's.

Are there any situations in your life today where you've given up and decided to keep crawling rather than go for what you really want, what you truly deserve? Have you lost the ability to make up a goal, go for it and get it? Why don't you do what you did when you were just a year old?

The answer is both simple and sad: somewhere along the way, you lost faith. **You became too grown-up to take baby steps, too sure you would never succeed to let yourself fail a few times first.** You gave up on the universal truth that simple little disciplines, done again and again over time, would move the biggest mountains.

You forgot what you used to know about the Slight Edge. You stepped off the path of mastery.

There is something treacherous about letting go of that childlike willingness to try and try again. Something insidiously dangerous about buying into the idea, "that'll never work for me." It is this: settling for less, settling for failure and giving up on baby steps soon becomes a habit. The first time you give up, it's painful. But the more you give up, the easier and easier it gets—and success recedes further and further from your grasp.

Can you guess why? That's right: it's the Slight Edge—working against you. Life is heavy ... welcome to the ninety-five percent!

But as always, all we need to do is turn the coin over to find the good news here: it is just as easy to step into the habit of succeeding, as it is to slip into the habit of failing. The longer you live, the easier it can get.

And you can step back onto the path of mastery any time you want.

Wanting

> *There is one quality which one must possess to win, and that is definiteness of purpose, the knowledge of what one wants, and a burning desire to possess it.*
> — Napoleon Hill, *Think and Grow Rich*

We all have visions of the way we'd like things to be that are different from the way they are. It could be something as simple as wishing we weighed ten pounds less, or something as far-reaching as wishing we could feed the millions of children around the world who go to bed hungry every night.

When I sat having my shoes polished in the Phoenix airport, I couldn't have stopped myself from having a vision of the shoeshine woman's success if I'd tried. I *wanted* her to be successful, so much that it ached.

It's that ache that we need look at now for a moment, the ache of *wanting*.

Having a dream is not always a matter of all roses and sweetness; ambitions, aspirations and desires can be uncomfortable, even painful.

The word "want" has two meanings. It can mean you desire something; it can also mean you lack something. And in a way, those aren't really two meanings; they're two sides of the same meaning. We tend to desire what we lack, and lack what we desire.

That means your dreams can be painful. Letting yourself become aware of what it is that you desire, but do not presently have, means experiencing the "lack" side of the coin as well as the "desire" side. It means becoming more fully aware of what you don't have. It means staring at your present reality with a sober eye and refusing to kid yourself. Noticing that you're not where you want to be can be uncomfortable.

Wanting hurts.

Here's an interesting thing: if putting voice to your fondest dreams can make you a little uncomfortable, it can also make everyone around you uncomfortable, and often far more so. Tell your five closest friends about your biggest ambition, and watch how many of them squirm! Why? Because showing them your want (desire) also reminds them of their want (lack).

This is one reason that when you are formulating goals and creating a vision for your future, it's important to be careful whom you share them with. It's natural to share your enthusiasm with everyone around you—and it's also useful to remember that people often tend to respond by raining on your parade. When they do, it's not out of malice or the conscious desire to blunt your excitement. More often, it's simply a form of self-defense. They'd rather not hear about the vision you have, because it reminds them of the one they've lost.

Closing the Gap

When you took an honest look at your life back in the previous chapter, rating yourself as being on the success curve or failure curve in different areas, you were painting a picture of where you are now. The diagram shows that as point A, and where you *could be*, your vision of what's possible for you in your life, as point B.

To the extent that there is a gap between points A and B, there is a natural tension between those two, like holding a magnet near a piece of iron. You can feel the magnet tugging at the iron—and you can feel your dreams (B) tugging at your present circumstances (A).

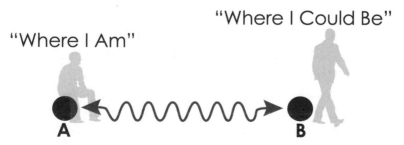

Tension is uncomfortable. That's why it sometimes makes people uncomfortable to hear about how things *could be*. One of the reasons Dr. Martin Luther King Jr.'s famous "I have a dream" speech made such a huge impact on the world and carved such a vivid place in our cultural memory is that it made the world of August 1963 very uncomfortable. John Lennon sang his vision of a more peaceful world in the song "Imagine"; within the decade, he was shot to death. Visions and visionaries make people uncomfortable.

These are of course especially dramatic examples, but the same principle applies to the personal dreams and goals of people we've never heard of. The same principle applies to everyone, including you and me.

Let's say you have a brother, or sister or old friend, with whom you had a falling out years ago. You wish you had a better relationship, that you talked more often, that you shared more personal experiences and conversations together. Between where you are today, and where you can imagine being, there is a gap. Can you feel it?

Or let's say you are a hard worker and make a pretty good income, but have no solid retirement plan and don't know how you'll be able to live comfortably when you reach your late sixties. There's how you'd *like* to be living at age sixty-eight, and how you're worried you *may end up* living at age sixty-eight if things go the way they're going. Between those two, there's a gap. Can you feel it?

Do you have any health or fitness goals? Career goals? Goals for your kids? Dreams of living somewhere else, of doing something else? Each of those images you have, of how things *could* be but at the moment are *not*, creates a gap with your present reality.

Most people, when confronted by problems larger than or of a different sort than they're already handling, immediately feel defeated or thrown off course. Most tend to see larger or different problems as negatives, and infect their own lives with negativity. What they don't realize is this philosophy: *The size of the problem determines the size of the person.*

You can gauge the limitations of a person's life by the size of the problems that get him or her down. **You can measure the impact a person's life has by the size of the problems he or she solves.**

If the size of the problems you solve is, "I put the cans in the bottom of the bag, and put the bread on top," as a grocery store bagger, that's the level of your problem solving and that's the level of your pay. If you can solve big problems, you can graduate to big pay—because the size of your income will be determined by the size of the problems you solve, too!

What most people call a "problem" is simply a gap, an open space between point A and point B. And if you keep an open mind, it's an open space you can bridge.

Now, here is the reason I've spent time describing and explaining this gap: *That gap can work against you or it can work for you.*

The gap between A and B cannot last forever. It has to resolve, and it will, one way or the other. It's a law of nature, and there's nothing you can do to stop it. But you do have a choice in how it resolves.

One way to resolve the tension is to move your point A (the way things are today) steadily closer and closer to point B. Let yourself be drawn by the magnet of your dreams, pulled along by the future. Remember what pulls those who dwell in the failure curve? The past. And what pulls people who live on the success curve? The future.

People who live with huge, vivid, clearly articulated dreams are pulled along toward those dreams with such force, they become practically unstoppable. What made people like Martin Luther King Jr., Gandhi or Mother Teresa, Edison or IBM's Thomas Watson, Wilberforce or Lincoln such forces of nature that nothing could stand in their way, no matter what the odds or obstacles? It was not some magic in their character, though they certainly became people of unusual character along the way. It was the power of their dreams. The vision each of these men and women held created a magnetic force against which no opposition could stand.

Again, I'm using dramatic examples of famous people, but the exact same thing occurs with people you and I have never heard of, everyday people who are not at all famous, but simply have dreams they care about and keep alive every day. That's the force you can harness in the pursuit of your own dreams.

What about the other direction? I said there were two ways that tension can resolve, and the other way is the one that works against you. If you don't close the gap by moving your present circumstance (A) constantly toward your goals and dreams (B), how else can you let the tension resolve?

Quit dreaming.

Just let go of all your dreams, goals, ambitions and aspirations. Settle for less. Make point B disappear, just delete it, and—*poof!*—the tension is gone. And that, sadly, is the choice that the ninety-five percent who travel the failure curve eventually make.

It's not hard to understand why so many people make that second choice. After all, when you're standing here at point A, gazing off into the distance at point B, it's easy to be intimidated by how far away it looks. People don't even want to set foot on the path if they don't think they can make it to the end. *Why even try? I mean, if the mountain's that huge, why take the first step? I'll probably never make it anyway* ... When the journey seems daunting, "easy not to do" can be a lot more appealing than "easy to do"!

But remember, you have to go one direction or the other; you can't stand still. Everything is constantly changing. There are only two possibilities. Either you let go of where you are and get to where you could be, or you hang onto where you are and give up where you could be. You are either going for your dreams or giving up your dreams. Stretching for what you could be, or settling for what you are. There is simply no in-between. Remember, this is the Slight Edge—and doing nothing means going down.

It's your choice.

The Deceptive Majority

> *All truth passes through three stages. First, it is ridiculed. Second, it is violently opposed. Third, it is accepted as being self-evident.*
>
> — Arthur Schopenhauer

Those two Slight Edge curves, the success curve and the failure curve, run parallel to each other for a long time. The two paths may be so close together that it's almost impossible for most people even to see the distinction between them. Then, all of a sudden, they veer away from each other, the success curve shooting up like an eagle and the failure curve plummeting downward like a stock market crash.

The people living on top, who take responsibility, live a life that is in some ways uncomfortable. Successful people do what unsuccessful people are not willing to do, and that often means living outside the limits of one's comfort zone. When you're one out of twenty, you're always going to be going in the opposite direction from the other nineteen.

The people on the other side are comfortable; they're with the masses. Their lives are more comfortable early on—but become more uncomfortable later on. Suddenly, late in life, they find they don't have the finances, don't have the health, no longer have the relationships, and their lives become very uncomfortable.

Those on the success curve, by contrast, end up far more comfortable later on, because they have the finances, the health, the relationships, the successes.

This means changing your thinking about the comfort zone. It's a change in philosophy. **It means embracing living uncomfortably in order to attain a life that is genuinely comfortable— not deceptively comfortable.**

The quote from Schopenhauer is a brilliant insight to the nature of the majority. The majority always let the first and second phases pass them by and wait until a truth is self-evident before signing on. What Schopenhauer is saying is the key to success is to identify things that are going to become self-evident *before* they're self-evident! Or to put it even more simply: find out what the majority is doing and do the opposite, which can be uncomfortable.

Of course, you have to apply some intelligence; you can't expect things to work just because they're in opposition to the majority. But the chances are excellent that when you step up onto the success curve, you will be stepping out alone. Like Wilberforce, Edison, Lincoln and Gandhi.

Do the opposite of the majority. Risk being the one, not one of the nineteen. Will people criticize you? Of course. **But have you ever seen a statue erected for a critic? We don't build statues for the ninety-five percent: we build them for the five percent.**

What I Learned from Funerals

At one point in my life, when I entered the corporate world and went to work for Texas Instruments, I was all ready to work my way up in management, but life had other plans for me. I showed up for work and they put me in sales.

I was horrified. I didn't want to be a salesperson. I hated sales. I didn't think I could do it. I *knew* I couldn't do it. What I had was not fear of rejection; it was *terror* of rejection. I knew what I would do—I would quit this job and go back to graduate school.

But successful people do what unsuccessful people are not willing to do. I was up against the wall: I *had* to do it and I knew it.

For my first sales call, I pored over the customer files and found the tiniest, most insignificant account I could: a tiny little drugstore in Gainesville, Florida. I figured that if I was going to make a mess, I might as well do as little damage as possible.

I drove for two and a half hours to arrive at that store, white-knuckled with fear. I parked and sat in the lot for a good half hour, leaning my face into the air conditioner vents (with the AC turned up full blast) and sweating buckets. I was terrified. Staying in that car would have been the easiest thing in the world to do right then. And on some level, even though I had not yet articulated the Slight Edge philosophy in my life, I knew that this simple little error, compounded over time, would rob me of all my dreams.

As I had prepared myself to go on this first sales call, I had been literally praying for help, and as so often happens when you ask a question in all sincerity, an answer came. In this case, it came in the form of an article I happened to read in a magazine.

The article was about funerals, and it informed me that at the average funeral, about ten people cry.

I couldn't believe it. *Ten people? That's it? You mean, I go through my entire life, spend years and years going through all these trials and tribulations and achievements and joys and heartbreaks—and at the end of it, there are only ten people who care enough to cry?*

I went on to the next paragraph. It got worse.

Once those ten (or fewer) people had yanked their hankies and honked their noses and my funeral was over, the number one factor that would determine how many people would go on from the funeral to attend the actual burial would be ... the weather. (The weather?!) If it happened to be raining, it said, fifty percent of the people who attend my funeral would decide not to go to my burial after all.

I really couldn't believe it. *You mean, I'm lying there, at the grand conclusion of everything I've ever said and done, of everything I call my life, in those final moments when my entire life is called to account and acknowledged and memorialized by those nearest and dearest to me, those whose lives I've most deeply and profoundly touched ... and half the congregation checks out halfway through because of the weather?!*

At first, this really bummed me out.

And then, it was liberating.

You know what? I thought. *I don't give a damn what anybody thinks of what I'm doing any more. If the odds are that iffy as to whether or not they even cry at my funeral, and chances are fifty-fifty that they duck out before I'm planted if the sky happens to cry for me more than the people do ... then why am I spending so much time worrying about what they're thinking now?*

Why would I be afraid of rejection? Why would I be concerned about what the majority thinks? Why would I be worried about what the ninety-five percent say, think, or do?

Facing some truths about one's own death can also bring one face to face with some important truths about one's life. Reading that article enlarged my comfort zone, and gave me an edge of courage—just a tiny edge, but an edge I hadn't had before. A Slight Edge.

I finally mustered what courage I could, turned off the car, went inside and gave what I am convinced to this day was the worst presentation in the history of sales. They did not buy a thing. In that sense, it was a total failure—but when I got back in my car, I was elated. I had blown the sales call, and had achieved a victory in my life.

A few days later, I happened to be thinking about that article as I sat in my car, stopped in traffic. Just then, I saw why we were all stopped: a funeral procession went by. It took less than a minute because it contained only a few cars.

As traffic slowly started moving again, I thought, *That person lived his or her entire life worrying about what other people thought ...*

And it suddenly hit me. Who has long funeral processions? At whose funerals do thousands cry? For whom do the millions mourn? For those who will do what others are not willing to do. For the people for whom we erect statues.

Martin Luther King Jr., Gandhi, Mother Teresa, Lincoln.

Gigantic funerals are held and great crowds, sometimes entire nations, mourn for those people who spent their lives not worrying about what others thought.

KEY POINTS OF CHAPTER 8

Mastery is not some vaulted, lofty place that only the elite few ever land. The pursuit of any aim, goal or dream—personal, professional, spiritual, in any area—is a Slight Edge journey of continuous improvement, learning and refinement. But mastery is not an exalted state that lies at the end of the path; it is a state of mind that lies at the very beginning. Mastery is the act of setting your foot on the path.

Shortly after my baby girl was born, I reluctantly turned to a state-run WIC program that provided milk for her—milk I couldn't afford to buy myself. It was a clear and defining moment in my life. I was in early 20's and my life was spiraling downwards fast in all categories: finances, family, fitness, faith, friends, fun and freedom.

Where I was in my life was based entirely upon the decisions I'd made over the last five years, and nearly every one of them lead me down the path of gradual decline. Deep down inside I knew I had to move from a life of entitlement to a life of responsibility.

One decision I made was critical. Every day while I was taking care of my baby girl, I would have a TV channel called *The People's Network* playing in the background. Whenever I fell off track, I would hear someone on that channel share some wisdom, some insights that helped get me get back on track.

Around that time I attended an event where Jeff Olson shared the Slight Edge concept, that he said had served him well in life, and then added, "I think it will do you well." I remember the words clearly. He shared how it's in the last 20 percent of the time we invest in a discipline, when all the rewards come. I needed something to believe in, so that day I bought into his belief in the Slight Edge philosophy.

I'll never forget those days of struggling—fall off track, get back on track, fall off track, get back on track. Realizing I was the project, I went to work on me. I read and applied what I learned. I went to work and I did my best. I applied long-term vision and delayed gratification.

I knew in order to be successful, I had to do what others were not willing do to themselves. If I became a success, it would be because of me. If I became a failure, it would be because of me. I couldn't blame anyone, I wouldn't and I didn't.

Was it easy? No. Was it worth it? ' You bet!

Over time I started to hit the magical "20 percent Slight Edge tipping point" mark in my finances, with my family, fitness, faith, friends, even fun and freedom followed.

Every decision I made over the next five years was a Slight-Edge decision, but this time it was a decision in simple disciplines, not simple errors in judgment. The majority of my decisions were now leading me down the path of growth.

I became living proof that the Slight Edge works. Since that time I've taught the Slight Edge philosophy to audiences in over twenty countries. I created a Slight Edge chart for myself, the same chart my daughter used to keep her on track to earning a black belt in the martial arts, the same one she used to develop the habit of reading 15 pages of a personal growth book a day, the same one she used to develop powerful critical thinking skills.

My daughter recently turned 18 and just left on a 90-day trip to Italy. I'm thrilled for her, and a bit sad. I miss her. And I know she'll be fine, after all, the Slight Edge philosophy is now part of her DNA. She also has a 3-year young sister. And yes, thanks to the Slight Edge, I can afford the milk this time around.

—Art Jonack, Houston TX

CHAPTER 9

Faces of the Slight Edge

The highest good is like water.

Water gives life to the ten thousand things and yet does not compete with them.

It flows in places that the mass of people detest and therefore is it close to the Way.

— Lao Tzu, *Tao Te Ching*

The Slight Edge is simple and constant. At the same time, the more you understand it and the more you become familiar with it, the more you will come to recognize its influence in your life in many forms and under many disguises.

It is the irresistible force delivered by the tidal wash that polishes the sharp edges of a rocky reef to porcelain smoothness; it is as ever-present in all aspects of life as the water molecule is in biology.

It is the force hiding within the music that "soothes the savage breast." Writing about love, the Apostle Paul said that it is a force that "endures all things and conquers all things," and within the universal human solvent of love, it's not hard to recognize the power of the Slight Edge. Mark Twain wrote, "Against the assault of laughter, nothing can stand." That is the power of the Slight Edge.

There are several faces of the Slight Edge I want to point out to you because they each represent a power that, once you recognize it in your life, you can harness in the pursuit of your dreams. They are momentum; completion; habit; reflection; and celebration.

Harness the Power of Momentum

Who won the race—the tortoise or the hare? We all know the answer to that one. Yet we live in a world where most everyone has come to expect instant this and instant that, and if we don't get the results we're after fast and faster, we quit.

Get rich quick. The fast lane. That fellow standing in front of the microwave muttering, "Hurry uppp, hurry uppp ... " Fast, faster, fastest is a strategy that will eventually take you *down* the Slight Edge curve.

M.I.T. professor Peter Senge puts this beautifully in his best-selling business book, *The Fifth Discipline—The Art & Practice of the Learning Organization*:

> *Virtually all natural systems, from ecosystems to animals to organizations, have intrinsically optimal rates of growth. The optimal rate is far less than the fastest possible growth. When growth becomes excessive—as it does in cancer—the system itself will seek to compensate by slowing down; perhaps putting the organization's survival at risk in the process.*

— Peter Senge, *The Fifth Discipline*

Have you ever witnessed something or someone that grew too fast? A business that expanded too rapidly and then self-destructed? A rock star, movie star or sports star who became a shooting star and went BOA—Burned Out on Arrival? Faster can end up being slower; too fast often puts the system's (or the person's) survival at risk.

Dr. Senge talks about "intrinsically optimal rates of growth"; **your optimal rate of growth is always served best by a step-by-step approach of constant, never-ending improvement, which lays solid foundations and builds upon them over and over.** The Slight Edge is your optimal rate of growth. Simple disciplines compounded over time. That's how the tortoise won; that's how you get to be a winner, too.

Having said that let me ask this: What is the real point of the story of the tortoise and the hare? Altogether now: *Slow and steady wins the race, right?* But notice something here: the point is not that there's any special virtue to moving slowly. There's nothing inherently good about slowness, and it's just as possible to move too slowly as to move too quickly.

The key word in the Aesop moral is not "slow"—it's *steady*.

Steady wins the race. That's the truth of it.

The fable of the tortoise and the hare is really about the remarkable power of momentum. A body at rest tends to stay at rest—and a body in motion tends to remain in motion. That's why your activity is so important. Once you're in motion, it's easy to keep on keeping on. Once you stop, it's hard to change from stop to go.

> *Be not afraid of going slowly;*
> *be afraid only of standing still.*
> — Chinese proverb

I coach people how to build large businesses by doing very simple, easy-to-do actions every day. I've found that it's far more effective to take one business-building action every day for a week, than to take seven, or ten, or even two dozen, all at once and then take the rest of the week off. People who do the first, week in and week out, build a solid business; people who do the second, don't—*even if they are actually doing a greater number of those business-building actions.*

Why not? No momentum. After six days off, they have to start all over again, getting themselves geared up and inspired to get back into action. It can take a good amount of energy and initiative to get yourself started in a new activity— but it takes far, far less to keep yourself doing it once you've started.

There's another reason once a day is better than seven times, once a week: the daily rhythm of the thing starts to change you. It becomes part of your routine, and as it does, it becomes part of who you are. That doesn't happen with a once-in-a-while, all-out effort.

Imagine taking a twenty-minute brisk walk in the morning, and then in the late afternoon, working out on a home gym for another twenty minutes. Now imagine that for a week, you did that every day. How would you feel at the end of the week?

Now instead, what if on that first day you had taken a 140-minute walk (that's over two hours!) and that afternoon, spent another 140 minutes on the home gym—and then done nothing for the next six days?

Steady wins the race.

When you're in motion, it's also far easier to make positive changes in your direction. It's like steering a car: when the car's sitting still, moving the wheel is hard work, but when it's moving, even at only 10 or 20 mph, turning is a breeze. It's a breeze because you're *already in the flow.*

Go Slow to Go Fast

The Slight Edge is a flow, and it moves at its own pace, automatically homing in on optimal growth rates. Part of understanding the Slight Edge is learning to go with the flow. **You can be as impatient as you like, but it won't bother the Slight Edge. It's always moving at its own optimal speed, with or without your consent, whether you are aware of it moving or not.** Dan Millman, in the book Way of the Peaceful Warrior (which is my favorite book), said it best when he said " Let it go and Let it flow."

To make the most of the Slight Edge flow, you'll want to match the speed of your growth and development to the natural progression of the Slight Edge. That's accomplished naturally by having a Slight Edge strategy.

It's easy to stay active. It's also easy not to. And if you stop, it won't kill you today—but, that simple error in judgment, compounded over time, will absolutely destroy the getting of any goal you're after.

Mary Kay Ash put this simply: *"Give yourself something to work toward constantly."*

Harness the Power of Completion

Another way you gather momentum and harness it to your advantage is by practicing an activity called *completion*.

Are there any things that are incomplete in your life? Any unpaid bills? Have you done your taxes? Did you borrow a book or tool you have yet to return? Is there someone who needs to hear you say, "I love you," or, "I'm sorry," or, "Thank you—I appreciate you"? Do you have any unfinished projects? Any unkept promises— taking a weekend away with your spouse, or taking your kids somewhere special? Are there any agreements or commitments you've left hanging?

Each and every incomplete thing in your life or work exerts a draining force on you, sucking the energy of accomplishment and success out of you as surely as a vampire stealing your blood. **Every incomplete promise, commitment and agreement saps your strength, because it blocks your momentum, inhibits your ability to move forward, to progress and improve. Incomplete things keep calling you back to the past to take care of them.**

Here's the unfortunate and powerfully destructive truth of being incomplete: it keeps the past alive. Remember, people who live on the success curve are pulled by the future, while those who dwell on the failure curve are pulled by the past. And a surefire way to be forced to live as a prisoner of your past is to not complete things.

Is it easy to do? Yes ... —wait. Let's consider that for a moment. No ... actually, it's *not* always easy to complete those incomplete things in life. Not when you've got a truckload of them to take care of. That stack of incompletions can loom larger than the Sears Tower. They can be absolutely overwhelming. Especially when you realize that whatever might have been keeping you from completing them in the first place—fear of confronting the issue, feeling intimidated or overwhelmed by it, worrying it might be difficult or uncomfortable—well, that's been compounded by the Slight Edge, too!

That's the Slight Edge working against you. That's how the pile got so big to begin with. And the truth is even those incompletions that seem difficult to do would have been a lot easier to do when they first came up than they might be now.

Approaching that stack of undones with the Slight Edge in hand is not only the best way to deal with them, it's the *only* way you'll ever deal with them. Take on those incompletions in your life just as you took on learning to walk. Baby steps, one at a time, letting the Slight Edge work for you to help you complete whatever needs completing.

Take on any one of your "incomplete" projects, one at a time. And if even that one project seems like too huge a mountain to climb, rummage around its foothills until you find an initial step you can take. The biggest meal is still eaten one bite at a time. Think of the title of Art Williams' best-seller, *All You Can Do Is All You Can Do, But All You Can Do Is Enough.* So find something you can do, and do that.

Make a phone call. Write a letter. Give fifteen minutes to completing something every day.

Read how *The Slight Edge* reader Valerie Thomas decided to tackle the "incomplete" project of her basement:

> I lived in a house with a huge unfinished basement that had 17 years' worth of clothes items, boxes, equipment, toys, you name it all around; there was one small path to walk to the back room to get to the washer and dryer. Eventually, time came when I had to move from that house and I thought I would never get to the basement. I cringed every time I thought of it. However after learning and applying the concept of the slight edge, I said that I would move/handle one bag or box every time I went to do clothes or get food. Before I knew it, I saw light; it looked easy to handle until eventually it was cleared out for a successful move.

What incomplete thing/project can you bring to completion?

Is it easy not to do? Absolutely. And if you don't do it today, will it destroy you? (You know the rest, so sing along ...)

Each time you do complete something, you get to move on with your luggage a little lighter and a bit more spring in your step.

Harness the Power of Habit

Sow an act, reap a habit;
Sow a habit, reap a character;
Sow a character, reap a destiny.

— Anonymous (attributed to various)

We often take habits for granted. There are bad habits you try to break but can't, good habits you wish you had but don't, annoying habits others have you wish they didn't, and odd habits you picked up yourself somewhere, for reasons totally mysterious to you. We're all aware that habits exist, though we often are not as aware of our own as others are.

However, **we seldom realize the enormous power of habits. There are two kinds of habits: those that serve you, and those that don't.** Brushing your teeth is a habit that serves you; biting your nails is one that doesn't. Thinking things through for yourself serves you; blindly accepting everything you read on the Internet or hear on television doesn't. Looking for the best in people serves you; anticipating their worst doesn't.

The first type of habit wields the force of the Slight Edge on your behalf and moves you along the success curve; the second turns the Slight Edge subtly but remorsefully against you and pulls you down the failure curve.

A habit is something you do without thinking. You come home from work, walk into the house, pull a beer out of the fridge and flick on the TV while you're talking to someone on the phone, without any conscious decision that a beer is exactly what you need right now or that there is something you urgently need to see on television.

Getting up early can become a habit. So can getting up late and staying up late. Complaining can become a habit. Spending more than you earn can become a habit; so can putting a piece of every paycheck into a retirement account. Looking for the positive side of every challenge can become a habit, so can finding the cloud in every silver lining.

The way a behavior turns into a habit is by repeating it over and over and over again until it becomes automatic. The creation of habits is a pure Slight Edge: simple little actions, repeated over time. The compounded effect of those habits over time will work either for you or against you, depending on whether they're habits that serve you, or habits that don't.

Your habits are what will propel you up the success curve
or down the failure curve. The individual who wants to
reach the top in business must appreciate the might of
the force of habit—and must understand that practices

are what create habits. He must be quick to break those habits that can break him—and hasten to adopt those practices that will become the habits that can help him achieve the success he desires.

— J. Paul Getty

It's interesting to note where your habits really come from. They arise out of your actions, true—but where do your actions come from? Remember this?

your **PHILOSOPHY** creates your **ATTITUDE** your **ACTIONS** your **RESULTS** creates your **LIFE**

Your habits come from your daily activities compounded over time. And your activities are the result of the choices you make in the moment. Your choices come from your habits of thought, which are the product of your thinking, which comes from the view you have of the world and your place in it—your philosophy.

Which is why the key to your success, to mastering the Slight Edge through the long-term effect of your everyday habits of thought and action, is your philosophy.

The point of this book is to give you a structure for designing your success. Once you are aware of and understand how to use the Slight Edge to work for you, you can go about succeeding on purpose. Your intuitive sense of the Slight Edge becomes your automatic pilot. It guides you, keeps you on track and helps you measure your progress. It weighs and measures your every habit, discarding those that don't serve you and designing new ones that do.

The key is making those right choices.

Each choice you make is like a length of steel wire. By itself, it's not that big a deal, but when braided together, when compounded with all the other choices you make, these lengths of wire form a thick cable of awesome strength and power.

Nothing is stronger than habit.

—Ovid

Have you ever seen the huge steel cables that hold up suspension bridges like the Golden Gate Bridge in San Francisco or the Verrazano Narrows Bridge in New York? They're flexible, yet they're so thick and strong you get the sense that no earthly force could break them. The cables made up of your right choices are just like those cables. So are the ones made from your wrong ones. The cables made from your right choices uphold and support you. Those made from wrong choices imprison and restrain you. These cables are your habits of thought and attitude.

Want to know where the Slight Edge is taking you? Look at your predominant habits of thought (my friend John Fogg calls them your "habitudes") and the kinds of choices you habitually make.

Your habits operate at the unconscious level; you are not normally aware of them. It's only by bringing a habit into your conscious awareness that you can observe what it's doing, how it empowers and serves you, or doesn't. By developing Slight Edge thinking (and especially by harnessing the next power we'll talk about, the power of reflection), you'll shine the bright light of awareness on your habits.

Once you're aware of a habit that doesn't serve you, how do you change it or get rid of it? It takes time—and it takes knowing where to focus your energy.

Trying to get rid of an unwanted habit is a bit like trying not to think about an elephant (the more you try not to think about it, the more you think about it). That's because what you focus on, grows. Which is why people who put a lot of energy into focusing on what they don't want, by talking about it, thinking about it, complaining about it or fretting about it, usually get precisely that unwanted thing.

It's tough to get rid of the habit you don't want by facing it head on. The way to accomplish it is to *replace* the unwanted habit with another habit that you do want. And creating new and better habits, ones that empower and serve you, is something you know how to do. You do it the same way you built any habit you have: one step at a time. Baby steps. The Slight Edge.

Harness the Power of Reflection

In my business, I often see people make the mistake of thinking they are being productive because they are being busy. **Being productive and being busy are not necessarily the same thing. Doing things won't create your success; *doing the right things will.*** And if you're doing the wrong things, doing more of them won't increase your odds of success—it will only make you fail faster!

Nobody sets out to fail. We all believe we're headed down the right path, or at least, a reasonably right one. People get out of bed, go to work and work hard. They love their families. They put smiles on their faces. They do everything they're supposed to do and they think they've had a productive day, or at least set out to have one. And all too often, what really happened is that they spent the day treading water like a duck swimming upriver against a strong current, its little webbed feet flailing away underneath but getting him nowhere.

Everybody's busy. Everyone does the actions. But were they the right actions? Were those actions productive? Did you take a step forward?

These are questions that most people never take the time to think about.

Did you eat well, or did you eat badly? Who did you associate with today? Did they empower you? How? In what way? Did you listen to good information today, or just zone out to the music? Did you engage in positive conversation, or did you gossip or complain? What did you read that contributed to your success today? Did you do any of the things unsuccessful people aren't willing to do? Whose dream did you build today—yours or somebody else's?

In the 12-Step System, this is called "taking a searching and fearless personal inventory." I honestly encourage you to get a little searching and fearless with yourself. Keep your progress—or the lack of it—in your face!

Here's a powerful exercise: Instead of writing down what you're *going* to do (chances are you've been doing that your entire life anyway, and it doesn't make you any better at doing them!), write down at the end of the day what you *did* do that day. What actions did you take today that made you successful?

Did you read ten pages of a good book? Did you eat healthy food and get some good exercise? Did you engage in positive associations? Did you do the things you need to do to be successful in your business? Did you tell somebody, "I love you"?

At the end of a week, look back over your lists and take inventory. Not only will it tell you a lot about the truth of your everyday life, chances are good that the mere act of recording this daily reflection will have already started changing what you do!

Here's what this exercise did for me the first time I did it: After the first few days, I found that by 10:00 in the morning, I was changing my normal course for the day and engaging in more positive Slight Edge actions—because I didn't want to face that man in the mirror empty-handed again that night!

There are lots of different ways to practice consistent self-reflection, and I don't necessarily recommend one over another, simply because everyone's different and what works best for me may not work best for you.

Some people accomplish this by keeping a journal. If you choose this approach, here's the key to making it work: don't just write down a record of what happened today, along with your thoughts and feelings about what happened. Ask yourself the specific Slight Edge questions. *In each area of my life, what are the critical, simple little things that are easy to do, and easy not to do? Did I do them? Did I move forward? Did I ride on the success curve?*

Some like keeping a journal sporadically, but find it difficult to keep up day in and day out, and instead create a specific, written list of Slight Edge actions that they consult and check off every day. On days they don't make time to write an entry in their journal, they at least go through the list and ask themselves those questions: *In each area of my life, did I do those things that are easy to do, and easy not to do? Did I continue my momentum on the success curve?*

Some would rather talk than write, and prefer to keep track of the day's actions out loud, in conversation. You can find a Slight Edge buddy, a friend who also wants to harness the power of reflection, and schedule a little time together or on the phone to debrief each other. *How did the day go? In each area of my life, did I ... ?* Doing this every day is ideal, but you can still make it work very well with a twice-a-week call, or even a once-a-week call. The key is consistency; like the tortoise, steady wins the race.

More and more, people are choosing to achieve a higher level of productivity through reflection by working with a coach. Only ten or fifteen years ago, most people thought of "coaching" only in the context of athletics. Then people realized that they had way better chances of pursuing their fitness goals if they used a personal trainer.

Soon, high-level business executives started using individual consulting sessions with productivity consultants to "coach" them in their high-stakes financial and organizational game. And in the last few years, the dam burst: people suddenly realized they could hire a coach for anything and everything, and the field of "personal coaching" exploded as one of the hottest new occupations.

So, what does a coach do? More than anything else, a coach holds up a mirror and shows you what you're doing, day in and day out. A coach keeps the Slight Edge in your face. A coach helps you harness the power of reflection.

Whatever method you choose to use, find some way to make reflection an everyday thing, day in and day out, without fail.

When what you didn't improve one day is clear to you and you're aware of it, by 10:00 the next morning you'll be hunting for self-improvements like a heat-seeking missile. You'll be reading, listening, associating to and with things and people that empower you. You won't be able to help it! You'll become so motivated that nothing—*nothing*—will prevent you from improving.

Harness the Power of Celebration

There is another critical reason the power of reflection is so important. It's not just to be a nag and remind you when you're slacking off. It's also to point out to you all the positive steps you're taking.

Over twenty years ago, authors Ken Blanchard and Spencer Johnson wrote, "People who feel good about themselves produce good results." The little book in which these words appeared, *The One Minute Manager*, became one of the decade's most influential business books. Blanchard and Johnson coined what has become one of the most well worn phrases in business: they urged managers and business owners not to walk around trying to catch people doing something wrong, but to "catch them doing something right," and then acknowledge it on the spot. They called this a "one minute praising."

It's easy to forget to catch yourself doing something right.

If you have kids, chances are that you can still remember the moment they took their first step. Chances are good that step got noticed and celebrated, big time. And chances are even better that within a week, they were walking around for hours a day and nobody even gave it a second thought—including them.

I heard a story once about a woman who had reached a point in her early fifties where she felt she was so badly starving for affection, she didn't know if she could continue in her marriage. She told her husband how she felt, and said that for years, she had been unable to tell if he still loved her or not.

Her husband was genuinely perplexed. "But I told you I love you thirty years ago," he exclaimed. "Why would you think anything changed?" Poor man: it had never occurred to him that it's not enough to say, "I love you" one time. It's something that needs saying every day, and not only in words, but in actions, too, especially those little, thoughtful things that say, "I'm thinking about you and I care about you."

It's the Slight Edge power of reflection and acknowledgement—celebration.

Keep your Slight Edge activities, your right choices and incremental successes, right out in the open where you can see them and celebrate them. Remember that all the activity ever required to apply the Slight Edge for your success is nothing but a series of baby steps. Trust the process. Acknowledge those steps, no matter how small or insignificant they may seem at the time.

Is it easy to do? Yes. Easy not to do? Yes. If you don't do it, will it destroy you? No ... but that simple error in judgment, compounded over time, will ruin your chances for success.

Make each successful right choice a celebration. You'll be able to feel, literally, those balance scales shifting in your favor. Nothing breeds success like more success.

KEY POINTS OF CHAPTER 9

There are several faces of the Slight Edge that, once you recognize it in your life, you can harness in the pursuit of your dreams.

Momentum—Steady wins the race. Once you're in motion, it's easy to keep on keeping on. Once you stop, it's hard to change from stop to go.

Completion—Each and every incomplete thing in your life or work exerts a draining force on you, sucking the energy of accomplishment and success out of you. Take on those incompletions in your life just as you took on learning to walk.

Habit—Your habits are what will propel you up the success curve or down the failure curve.

Reflection—Being productive and being busy are not necessarily the same thing. Doing things won't create your success; doing the right things will. Were those actions productive? Did you take a step forward?

Celebration—Keep your Slight Edge activities, your right choices and incremental successes, right out in the open where you can see them and celebrate them. Acknowledge those steps, no matter how small or insignificant they may seem at the time.

When we were first introduced to the Slight Edge principles we were financially upside down. We did not have the ability to pay our own bills, let alone bless the lives of others. After understanding the Slight Edge philosophy we started applying it to every area of our lives. We applied the principles to our family business. As a team we focused on daily activities that we knew would eventually give us the momentum we needed to achieve our goals. We made sure we completed tasks and did what we said we would do so that nothing could hold us back to the past.

We spent time reflecting on how our efforts could be more productive as a team and we looked for every opportunity to celebrate our success as well as recognize others that helped us gain those successes. The results of applying those principles have been more than we could have imagined. Our income grew 1,000 pecent in just 5 years. I guess you could say we put in our 10,000 hours and it was definitely worth it.

Beyond that, we have been able to start a non-profit foundation to help the less fortunate. Our proudest accomplishment has been recently raising over $100,000 for a girls orphanage in Guatemala. We have also begun to organize trips every 90 days for others to volunteer at the orphanages. By implementing these simple principles into our lives we have not only drastically improved the quality of our lives, but more importantly have been able to reach out and touch those in need.

—Mike, Steve, & Kim Melia, Wilmington, NC

CHAPTER 10

Invest in Yourself

> *No stream rises higher than its source. Whatever*
> *man might build could never express or reflect more*
> *than he was. He could record neither more nor less*
> *than he had learned of life when the buildings were*
> *built ... His philosophy, true or false, is there.*
>
> — Frank Lloyd Wright

The greatest gift you could ever give yourself is also the wisest business investment you could ever make. It is also the most critical step in accomplishing any challenging task, and is the one step without which all other success strategies, no matter how brilliant or time-tested, are doomed to fail.

What is this mysterious gift? It is *your own personal development.* Investing in your own improvement, your own personal growth and betterment, is all these things and more.

Abraham Lincoln said, "Give me six hours to chop down a tree, and I will spend the first four hours sharpening the axe." In other words, he would spend twice as much time working on himself as on the task itself.

What do most people do? They grab the axe, dull or not, and start whaling away at the tree. And if they aren't making a major dent in that tree pretty soon, they quit—and probably mutter something about how it's the tree's fault!

How you swing the axe, how hard, in what arc and with what rhythm on exactly what spot you hit the tree—all these are strategies that concern your actions, and they can all be measured, weighed, and improved ... but it starts with the axe itself. And the axe is you.

Results Come Last

It is easy to be seduced by the promise of results. We live in a results-oriented world, a culture that overwhelmingly measures the success of a course of action by its results. Talk is cheap, after all—and what is it that really matters? Results. The bottom line. Show me. Proof of the pudding's in the eating, right?

But there is a problem here. There's a flaw in this thinking. In fact, the flaw in this thinking is so profound; ninety-five percent of all people's efforts are ending up as failure! And what is so remarkable is that this isn't some deep, hidden, subtle flaw. It's so obvious, everyone ought to see it—but it's so deeply ingrained in our culture, nearly everyone is hypnotized into missing it.

Here is the flaw: **How can you judge the course of action you're taking by its results, when its results come last?**

The problem with focusing on results is simply that it doesn't work. Having your attention on your results is like driving your car by looking in the rearview mirror. Your results live in the past, and like all things in the past, they belong there.

What you can do with your results is learn from them. Results are valuable feedback. Let them help motivate and guide your tomorrows. But a focus on results only takes you out of the present moment where the action really is.

What about your actions?

Many approaches to personal and professional development I have observed go deeper than results by focusing instead on your actions as the place to bring about positive change. That's a logical place to start looking, but the problem is that your actions are not the source of your success or failure.

Again, that's why diets don't work; they can't. They're doomed to fail because most diets dictate what your actions should be. They don't deal with where your actions come from.

The only reliable, consistent way to control your attitudes—that control your actions, which control your results—is to control your thoughts. And the source of your thoughts is your philosophy. This is why the master entrepreneur W. Clement Stone uttered these often-quoted words: "What the mind of man can conceive and believe, the mind of man can achieve."

Your philosophy is your paradigm, your view of the way life is. It is how you say life works or doesn't work, and determines everything about the course of actions you'll choose and *keep choosing over time*. **Your philosophy is the foundation upon which you build your life. There is nothing more fundamental or essential.**

Your philosophy is the source of your failure or success. It is the garden in which your beliefs grow—and your beliefs lay the fertile groundwork for everything else. The Slight Edge will either promote you or expose you for who and what you really are—and who and what you are comes from your philosophy.

In the Sermon on the Mount, Jesus spoke of two types of foundation. He spoke about the "wise man" who built his house upon the rock: "And the rain descended, and the floods came, and the winds blew, and burst against that house; and yet it did not fall, for it had been founded upon the rock."

And then he told of a second character—a "foolish man" who built his house on sand: "And the rain descended, and the floods came, and the winds blew, and burst against that house; and it fell and great was its fall."

The foundation upon which you are building the house of your life is what will determine the nature of the house itself. Will the house stand? Will it fall apart? Will it leak, or will it withstand whatever weather nature throws at it? What results will your life produce? It's a critically important question—because by the time the results are in, the outcome will already be pretty well determined. You can't wait for your results to judge your actions. You can't wait to see what kind of house you've got before you judge whether or not it had a sturdy foundation!

Your success will always be the *progressive realization* of a worthy ideal. Your philosophy comes first; your results come last. And this brings us to the most important Slight Edge strategy of all.

Continuous Learning

> *The trouble with the world is not that people know too little, but that they know so many things that ain't so.*
> — Mark Twain

We've talked about all sorts of forces you can harness to help power your path through life. The most important force of all, the force that drives the whole process of living with the Slight Edge, is the power of *continuous learning*.

When I say "learning," I don't mean simply learning from school, although schooling certainly has its place. And I don't just mean learning from books or from a teacher—though you already know that I revere the knowledge to be gained from good books, and I feel the same way about great teachers, too. I'm also not just talking here about learning from the example of others, from advice from your friends, from the "school of hard knocks," or learning from your mistakes ...

I don't mean any one of those ... I mean *all* of them! Once you've set foot on the path of mastery and grasped the philosophy of the Slight Edge, educating yourself through any and all means available is the critical process that will keep you on that path and make the Slight Edge work for you.

I also don't mean "education" in the more narrowly defined sense of learning specific skills or subjects. Naturally, you need to pursue continuous learning in order to acquire the knowledge and skills involved in mastering any subject or pursuit that will contribute to your personal and professional growth and development. But it's more than simply a matter of acquiring specific knowledge. Continuous, lifelong learning is the material from which you continually build your philosophy—and by now, you and I both know how important that is! Learning is also the material from which you build your awareness, and that is also critical in mastering the Slight Edge.

After getting out of high school, fifty-eight percent of all high school graduates who don't go on to college *never read a book again!* When I first read that figure, I was shocked ... but not surprised. That's one reason the ninety-five percent give up and slide down the failure curve. They spend their lives building someone else's dream, not because they aren't capable of building their own, but because they never gained the knowledge they needed.

Illiteracy is a much greater problem today than many people realize. Of the slightly more than six billion people on earth, according to the Wycliffe organization, one billion cannot read! Can you imagine that?! One person out of every six—one *billion* people—cannot read, and that rate is on the rise.

But consider this: If you are one of that fifty-eight percent who never reads after high school, what's the difference between you and the billion people around the world who couldn't read if they wanted to? No difference at all.

Of course, simply reading won't necessarily put you on the success curve. Remember my shoeshine woman and her little pile of novels? No question about her literacy—the woman loved to read. But where would she have been if that pile had included Norman Vincent Peale, Dale Carnegie, Zig Ziglar, Jim Rohn, *The Millionaire Next Door, Smart Women Finish Rich,* and any of the hundreds and thousands of other inspirational, educational, empowering books out there? Where would she have been if for the previous year or two, she'd read just ten pages, one chapter, of those books in between customers?

You know where she'd be.

When was the last time you attended a seminar or took an adult-education class, not because you were required to, but simply to improve yourself? When was the last time you went bowling? If your bowling average is over 200, congratulations! You're a heck of a bowler—and you may want to rethink your priorities. If you lined up the one hundred most successful men and women in America and calculated their bowling averages, I bet they wouldn't break 70. The average American will go bowling 233 times in his or her life—and they all have something better to do. I know bowling is one of the most popular pastimes in the United States, but wouldn't you rather have success be your most popular pastime?

I'm not picking on bowling, or any other form of recreation. We need balance in our lives, and taking time at the bowling alley can also serve you in all sorts of ways—your fitness, your relationships with your friends, your ability to let work go, to relax and have fun. All good things ... but the question is, are you developing yourself? Are you building your dream or only your boss's?

Read just one chapter of an information-rich, inspiring book every day. Listen to fifteen minutes of a life-transforming CD or audio download. Take a course or seminar every few weeks or months.

Are these things easy to do? Sure. And those simple disciplines compounded over time, like a penny doubled every day for a month, will send you up to the top. Are they easy not to do? No question. And if you don't do them, will you destroy your life today? Of course not. But that simple error in judgment, compounded over time, will pull you down the curve of failure and take away everything you've hoped for and dreamed about ... forever!

"Book Smarts" vs. "Street Smarts"

Q: Five frogs sat on a lily pad. One decided to jump off. How many were left?

A: Five ... all of them are still sitting there. The one frog only *decided* to jump.

The famous Chinese proverb says, "The journey of a thousand miles starts with a single step"—another wonderful example of traditional Slight Edge wisdom. But note: The journey starts with a single step—not with *thinking* about taking a step!

Plenty of people accumulate knowledge but still dwell on the failure curve. It's not only the quantity of knowledge that sets and keeps your course, but also the quality of knowledge. There are different types of knowledge and different avenues of learning; if you want to stay grounded and move ahead at the same time, you need a balance.

There are three principle kinds of learning. The first is *learning by study*, which includes reading, listening to CDs and audio downloads, and attending classes and seminars. The second type is *learning by doing*.

As passionate as I am about improving yourself by studying with great teachers, through great books, CDs and other media, I also know that all the study in the world won't build your business, establish your health, or create a happy, fulfilling family life. That takes your getting up and *doing it*. Book smarts is not enough: all true success is built from a foundation of study plus street smarts.

Life is not a spectator sport—it is a contact sport; there is no practice session. You've been immersed in it from day one; life lives in the right-here, right-now. That's why Emerson, who was an exceptionally well-educated man in the traditional book-smarts sense, advised, *Do the thing, and you shall have the power.*

Note that this is not a reversible philosophy. You can't just go get the power and *then* do the thing—though people do try to do it that way, and they spend their entire lives gathering the power ... and doing nothing.

Do the thing, and you shall have the power. The only way to have the power is to do the thing. Just do it. That's learning by doing.

In my marketing business, I'm often asked for the key to success. "What's the one thing I can do to guarantee my success?" My answer is always the same: "Be here, actively immersed in the process, one year from now." That's really the only right answer. It's the Slight Edge answer. You can't build your dream by what you're going to do or planning to do or intend to do. You only build your dream by building it.

If you aren't doing, you're dying. Life *is* doing.

The Rhythm of Learning

Knowledge without practice is useless. Practice without knowledge is dangerous.

— Confucius

I can read a book like *As a Man Thinketh*, return it to my bookshelf, then come back a year later to read it again—and it feels like somebody sneaked into my room while I was sleeping and completely rewrote the book! Why? Because of the learning by doing I've gone through in the interim. My experiences have changed my perspective. Now, when I read a particular passage or point the author makes, I understand it in a way I could not have possibly seen a year ago. And that in turn informs my behavior: now, when I go to engage in my activity of the next day, I can apply what I've learned from James Allen in a way that I would not have thought of even twenty-four hours ago.

Book smarts, street smarts. Learning by study, learning by doing. Read about it, apply it, see it in action, take that practical experience back to my reading, deepen my understanding, take that deeper understanding back to my activity ... it's a never-ending cycle, each aspect of learning feeding the other. Like climbing a ladder: right foot, left foot, right foot, left foot.

Can you imagine trying to climb a ladder with only your right foot?

The two work together. What's more, they not only work better together, each amplifying the other, but the truth is, they really cannot work separately. At least not for long.

You can't excel based purely on knowledge learned in study; you can't excel purely through knowledge gleaned through action. The two have to work together. You study, and then you do activity. The activity changes your frame of reference, and now you are in a place where you can learn more. Then you learn more, and it gives you more insight into what you experienced in your activity, so now you re-approach activity with more insight. And back and forth, it goes.

This back-and-forth rhythm is worth noting. It is the rhythm of success.

Remember when we talked about "baby steps"? This learning-and-doing sense of rhythm is something you learned even before you learned to walk, and it's even more basic. Psychologists have found crawling is one of the most important activities we ever accomplish, because it profoundly affects the brain and its capacity to learn. The right-hand-left-leg, left-hand-right-leg rhythm of alternation acts upon our nervous systems like the surf upon the coastline, developing it, shaping it, and preparing it for all sorts of more sophisticated levels of learning and awareness later in life.

You've heard the expression, "Before you can walk, you have to crawl." There is more profound truth to this than most of us ever realized. That alternating rhythm, and your capacity to coordinate the behavior of opposites, is a critical Slight Edge skill. Balancing book smarts and street smarts is one aspect of that, and so is the daily success strategy that we'll look at next: course correction.

Course Correction

> *You return again and again take the proper course—guided by what? By the picture in mind of the place you are headed for ...*
> — John McDonald

What's the shortest path between two points? A straight line, right? Wrong. While that might be true in theory, it's never true in reality. And reality is where you and I live—and where we succeed or fail.

Have you driven on any roads lately that are perfectly straight? Even when you're on one of those interstates that seems like a long straight line to forever, do you hold the steering wheel perfectly still? Or do you move it back and forth, constantly correcting the direction the car is headed? That constant moving of the steering wheel is so familiar, it's second nature, and you probably never think about it. But if you decided to hold the wheel rigidly in place, you'd be off the road, probably in less than a minute.

And in case you think that's just a matter of engineering, or of imperfections in the road's surface, this next example may come as a bit of a shock:

On its way to the moon, the miracle of modern engineering that is an Apollo rocket is actually on course only two or three percent of the time; for at least ninety-seven percent of the time it takes to get from the Earth to the moon, it's *off course*. In a journey of nearly a quarter of a million miles, the vehicle is on track for only 7,500 miles ... or to put it another way, for every half-hour the ship is in flight, it is on course for less than sixty seconds!

And it gets to the moon?! How is that possible?

Because modern space travel is a masterful example of the Slight Edge course correction in action.

If this machine, one of the most sophisticated, expensive and finely calibrated pieces of technology ever devised, was correcting its own off-course errors twenty-nine minutes out of every thirty, is it reasonable to expect that you could do better than that? And even if you were able to match the rocket's degree of accuracy, you'd still be perfectly on target, on track and on course no more than ten days *per year!*

For anyone who lacks a grasp of the Slight Edge, being off course is something to be avoided at all costs. After all, if you're off course, you're failing, right? But those who understand the Slight Edge embrace Thomas Watson's philosophy about failure. Here is a more extended version of what he said:

> *Would you like me to give you the formula for success? It's quite simple, really. Double your rate of failure ... You're thinking of failure as the enemy of success. But it isn't at all ... You can be discouraged by failure—or you can learn from it. So go ahead and make mistakes. Make all you can. Because, remember, that's where you'll find success. On the other side of failure.*

— Thomas J. Watson, Sr.

Remember, the rocket got there. And so can you. Why? Because of continuous course correction.

What enabled the rocket to continue to make those adjustments that brought it back on track to reach its destination? The adjustments were all done by a computerized guidance system, the heart of which was a gyroscope.

A gyroscope is a spinning mass mounted in a base that retains the same orientation no matter in what direction the base itself is going. You may have played with a toy gyroscope as a child—the kind you wind up with a string like a top, make it spin, and no matter how you hold it or what you do to it, it remains upright as long as it's spinning around. The force created by that toy gyroscope is so powerful it can balance on the tip of your finger or dance upright along a string.

The rocket starts from point A (its current position) and heads for point B (the moon). As it travels its first few miles, it gets slightly off course. Now the rocket's gyroscope shows one reading, while the rocket's instruments show that it's actually headed in a slightly different direction. The gyroscope, remember, is always pointed in the *right* direction, the direction the ship actually wants to go.

The computer processor detects that the rocket's off course and tells it to make an adjustment. If the processor and the rocket were speaking English, the conversation might sound something like this:

Processor: "Rocket, you're 1.27 degrees north—bring it back to 1.29."

Rocket: "Okay ... done."

Processor: "Good ... Whoa, that's too much, now you're 1.30— move it 0.01 degrees south."

Rocket: "No problem, I'll do that, too."

Processor: "Great—no, wait, too far west. Adjust course 0.067 degrees."

Rocket: "Got it, consider it done."

Processor: "Whoops, too much, come back 0.012."

Rocket: "Right, 0.012 ... how's that?"

Processor: "Little too far north again, ease back to 1.27 ... "

And so it goes, from here to the moon, a constantly occurring series of adjustments turning what is predominantly a string of failures into ultimate success.

You have a gyroscope, too, and it works in much the same way, if you allow it to. Your gyroscope is your vision of where you're going—in other words, your dream. Your processor is the Slight Edge: a consistent series of tiny, seemingly insignificant actions, easy to do and easy not to do, and in this case, doing them leads you directly to the moon instead of shooting off into the vacuum of outer space.

You're hungry. There's a bunch of greasy junk food in a vending machine beckoning you. Your gyroscope is spinning—it's focused on your health. Your processor goes, *click ... click ... whirr ...* and you choose a salad or a piece of fruit instead.

There's a display rack of books and magazines. You reach toward the copy of *People* because it has a juicy piece of gossip you'd just love to read—about a movie star you can't stand but it looks really intriguing anyway—and it's only a few bucks and you've got some time over lunch, and—*Click ... whirrr ... click ...* and instead you decide to go back to your car for your copy of *Smart Women Finish Rich*. Or to take a twenty-minute walk in the park.

You're having coffee with friends and they start complaining about their work, their bosses, their jobs ... *Click ... click ... whirrr ...* and you find a way to change the subject because you know that if the talk doesn't get onto a positive track within another sixty seconds, you'll find a reason to excuse yourself.

Click ... click ... whirrr ...

Knowing the Slight Edge, you make the adjustment automatically. You make those right choices, the ones that serve you. You do those simple, seemingly insignificant things that forward your progress up the success curve. You read good books. You listen to motivating tapes. You hang around successful people who empower you. You're a five percenter, a winner, a success.

Once you know the Slight Edge, you know that in getting from point A to point B you'll be off track most of the time. And you know that it's the adjustments—those little, seemingly insignificant corrections in direction—that have the most power in your life.

Kaizen: Plan, Do, Review

You know this saying: "Ready ... aim ... " and what comes next? "Fire!" right? That's the way it's usually put—but there's a better way.

Ready, fire, aim!

The problem with "Ready, aim, fire" is that in the real world, where everything is in motion and things are constantly changing, by the time you've finished all that readying and aiming, the target is long gone!

Here's another way of saying *ready, fire, aim*: plan, do, review.

"Plan, do, review" is an approach to learning that began gaining credibility in educational institutions toward the end of the twentieth century, and it's used in some of the better schools today. It's a Slight Edge strategy.

Students *plan* what they're going to learn and create their own activities and experiments for study. Then, they *do* what they planned. And then they *review* their planning and doing to see if anything was missing to help them learn what could be done to improve the process and the results they've accomplished. Then they plug those new insights into their next plan, and they're off and running up the Slight Edge curve to success.

The operative Slight Edge strategy at work here is the constant and consistent back-and-forth of doing actions and correcting those actions—course correction, just like the moon rocket. What this strategy produces is what business management philosophy has come to call "continuous improvement," a concept that the Japanese call *kaizen*.

This idea was introduced to Japan after World War II by an American, W. Edwards Deming. A remarkable statistician, Dr. Deming consulted and lectured Japanese industrial leaders about "total quality." He taught that "the system is the solution"—and showed how it's always the source of the problem as well.

Remember what happened to the Japanese and American auto industries in the '70s and '80s? The Japanese ate America's lunch in the marketplace. Know why? Slight Edge strategy. They had it; we didn't.

The Japanese took Deming's Slight Edge teachings about simple little disciplines in improving quality, compounded them over time, and in less than a decade they blew the much larger, richer and more powerful industry leader (the United States) out of the water. So far out of the water, in fact, that the top-selling car in America for years was the Honda.

It wasn't that the Americans didn't improve. The 1983 Chevy was clearly superior to the 1973 Chevy. But General Motors kept looking for those big breakthroughs, while the Japanese kept making little, seemingly insignificant improvements which, compounded over time, enabled them to steal the spotlight in what was once almost exclusively an American car show. The Japanese had major automotive breakthroughs, too, but they were the result of their Slight Edge strategy.

In the 1990s, the American auto industry made quite a comeback: great cars, record sales and profits. It was a stunning turnaround, and what turned it around were our automakers finally embracing the teachings of W. Edwards Deming: that a commitment to developing and sticking to a Slight Edge strategy will absolutely, positively send you to the top.

Plan, do, review (and *ready, fire, aim!*) creates a structure and support system for continuously improving. It's the strategy of constant course correction. You may have heard the expression, "It's not how you plan your work, it's how you work your plan." Not quite. A Slight Edge strategy means doing both at once— one tiny, course-correcting step at a time.

The Slight Edge is the process. You choose which way it goes: up with the five percent, or down with the other ninety-five percent. You don't just make that choice once and then say, "Ahh, I'm finished, now I'm all set." You make that choice moment to moment to moment—and keep making it, every month and every day, for the rest of your life.

Each new moment will present you with a new Slight Edge choice to be made. Before long it will become natural and automatic, but when you first begin, it will require your constant awareness.

You have to choose to make the Slight Edge work *for* you—moment by moment, one step at a time. Remember the rocket to the moon.

Is it easy to do? Yes. Is it easy not to do? Of course. If you don't do it, will your life collapse? No—not today. But that simple error in judgment, compounded over time, will pull you down the failure curve, absolutely and irrevocably, no questions asked. Unless you accept the wealthy man's third gift—the choice— and keep on accepting it, day by day and moment by moment.

Learning Through Modeling

Earlier I mentioned that there are three principal types of learning. We've examined the first two (learning through study and learning through doing) and you're probably wondering if we we're ever going to get around to the third! In a way, I've saved the best for last, because utilizing this third type of learning will tremendously accelerate the first two.

It is *knowledge through modeling.*

Throughout human history (and long before there were such things as books, universities or continuing education programs) there has been one tried-and-true path for learning a skill, craft, art, trade or profession: go study with a master. All the great learning traditions say the same thing: if you want to learn how to do something well, go find a master of that skill and apprentice yourself.

Like the "coaching" model, the "mentor/apprentice" model is experiencing a tremendous surge in popularity right now. Mentoring networks, agencies and organizations are springing up in all sorts of professions—and this doesn't surprise me in the least.

With the advent of the Internet culture, there's been an explosion in information over the past decade. Now we're starting to realize that information alone is not enough—and information plus personal experience (the "school of hard knocks") is not enough. We need some way to process all that information and experience and integrate it. And there is only one reliable, solid way to do that: find someone else or a community of people who have already mastered an area, and model yourself based on their experience.

A lack of community is the largest criticism of "personal development," as listed in Wikipedia's definition. Your personal development has to be a contact sport where you are in contact with others that can help you on your journey.

It has already been proven that information and technology alone are not going to create real change. Today, we see information on health soaring and yet we have seen an increase in obesity, adult onset diabetes, and other preventable diseases. We see information on finances everywhere, yet a rise in debt and mismanaged money. Information needs to be coupled with a community to have any real life-changing effects.

Let's look at an example where information and community are coupled together to create real change in people's lives.

Alcoholics Anonymous (AA) is a successful rehabilitation program because it provides all the information needed on the condition *and* marries that with a community of people to support the member. If it only handed out DVDs and brochures and put up a website about the disease, and left it at that, how many people do you think would actually recover? Not many. Of course, a member needs the information, but what makes the program truly work is the environment and associations that are created around that person. The same is true for personal development and any change we want to see in our life. It has to consist of information and a supportive environment.

Whatever goals you aspire to, just seek out people who have achieved the same or very similar goals, or who are well along that path, and go camp on their doorsteps or do whatever you can to associate with them, emulate them, and let their grasp, understanding and mastery of the subject rub off on you.

Spend Time with the Masters

If you want to raise the quality of your life, hang out with people who have been there and done that. If you want to be a great public speaker, spend time with great speakers. If you want to be a success in business, then find a way to spend time in the company of successful businesspeople. If it's important to you to be a terrific parent, the best thing you can do to further that aim is to spend lots of time with men and women who have mastered parenting.

You can define a society by the heroes it keeps. You can also define a person by the heroes he or she keeps. Who are your heroes? Who are you modeling yourself after?

The ninety-five percent on the failure curve tend to accept the heroes society plants in front of them: film stars (America's version of royalty), rock stars, sports stars. I can certainly admire these folks, but I always ask myself, *Can I emulate them?* Practically speaking, can I convert my admiration into constructive modeling that increases my learning and moves my own life forward?

Too often, we make heroes out of people who can't help us, whose lives are fantasies, not genuine role models. Take a look at who your heroes are—write down a list and examine it. Ask yourself, "Can I become like them? Are these people doing the kinds of things that I aspire to do and living the kinds of lives that I aspire to live? Can they really help me become who I want to become?"

Find people who've done what you want to do and surround yourself with them. That's learning through modeling, and it's a powerful part of learning how to understand and use the Slight Edge. Once you become worthy of being modeled, you in essence become the teacher. And if you teach long enough, people begin to look at you as a master.

The problem is that most people want to go from learning to becoming the teacher. They don't want to bother with having to learn the activities well enough to be modeled.

The quarterback position in football is a great example. First he has to learn the playbook. Secondly, he takes those plays from the chalkboard to the practice field. And if he is good enough at implementing his learned knowledge, the team eventually looks to him as a leader. If he is a worthy leader long enough, soon other team members are modeling him. When you watch great quarterbacks play like Joe Montana or Peyton Manning, it is very clear that they have been leaders of their team long enough that they have earned the right to be modeled after and are seen as the coaches on the field.

The Law of Associations

Do you remember a comment I made about income, way back in the very beginning of this book? While I was sitting in the Phoenix airport thinking about my new friend, the shoeshine woman, I mused over this thought:

Your income tends to equal the average of the incomes of your five best friends.

This principle does not apply solely to your finances: it operates in every aspect of your life.

Your level of health will tend to be about the average level of health of your five best friends. Your personal development will be at about the average level of personal development of your five best friends. Your relationships, financial health, attitudes, level of success in your career, and everything else about your life will tend to be very close to the average level of each of these conditions in your five closest friends and associates.

We all understand this principle instinctively; our language is shot through with idioms that reflect it:

You're known by the company you keep.

Show me where you fish and I'll show you what you catch.

Birds of a feather flock together.

You are the combined average of the five people you associate with most—including the way you walk, talk, act, think and dress. Your income, your accomplishments, even your values and philosophy will reflect them.

If the five people around you have negative philosophies, it's virtually impossible for you to have a positive philosophy. If the five people around you are consistently complaining, living in the past, blaming others for their difficulties, and thinking and acting in a generally negative way, then what are the odds of you finding your way onto the success curve? Slim to none.

If you consistently associate with negative people, it's highly unlikely you will succeed at having and maintaining a positive approach to your life.

Become acutely aware of who you are modeling. This has everything to do with your philosophy and your attitudes, which has more to do with your actions and with what you're actually doing and creating in your everyday life than any other factor.

The reason "birds of a feather flock together" is simply that they're all going in the same direction, headed for the same destination. Look at the people with whom you flock, the *company you keep*: what destination are they headed for? And is that where you want to be headed?

Look at the people around you. Are they more successful than you are? Are they people who live the kinds of lives you aspire to live, or the kinds of lives you hope to leave behind? On what side of the Slight Edge are they living—on the success curve or the failure curve? Is the Slight Edge working for them or against them? Where will they be in twenty years? And are they pulling you up or dragging you down?

This is a pass or fail test: there is no "maybe" about it. Remember, there is no standing still: we're all going in one of two directions, either up or down. Your association with each person you know is either empowering you, or it's not—taking you up the success curve or down the failure curve.

How can you tell? One way is to go back to the business of future and past, responsibility and blame. When you and this particular friend get together, are your conversations about responsibility, aspirations and taking initiative? Or do they often seem to work their way around to blame or its cousins—envy, jealousy, resentment and irritation?

Do your conversations focus more on the future or on the past? It's only natural, when you share a common history and set of experiences, to enjoy reminiscing over fond memories; that's not what I mean. What I mean is, does your relationship have a forward-looking, positive feeling to it, or do the two of you get together and always seem to end up circling events of the past, like a cat endlessly turning round and round before it can settle down to sleep?

If your relationship with someone has a theme of blame and feeds on the past, it's disempowering. If it has a theme of responsibility, self-reflection and change and feels like something moving into the future, it's empowering.

We are all either building our own dreams or building somebody else's. To put a finer point on it, we're either building our dreams—or building our nightmares.

There may be some people with whom you're now spending two days a week, where you might decide you need to take that down to two hours. There may also be people with whom you're spending only two minutes, where you'll realize you need to spend far more time with them—two hours or two days. And you will find times when what you really need to do is simply disassociate yourself from someone; that's a part of the Law of Association, too.

For many people, I think this can be a tough aspect of the Slight Edge to understand and accept. Most everything else about the Slight Edge, as you already know, is easy to do—but disassociating yourself from people who do not empower you can be a sad and difficult thing to do. Especially if you love them. Especially if they are old friends or dear family.

So take heart: by "disassociating," I don't necessarily mean cutting them out of your life completely. But casual relationships deserve casual time—not quality time. There are people with whom you can spend two minutes, but not two hours. There are people with whom you can spend two hours, but not two days.

This part of Slight Edge thinking requires a compassionate *awareness*. Having compassion and having direction are not mutually exclusive: they just take careful thought and discernment. You're not judging those people; you're simply asking yourself to be honest about whether or not those relationships are empowering you and helping to support your purpose and realize your dreams.

Leadership

I'm often asked, "How do I become a leader?" In our push-button, instant-everything world, like I said before, people often seem to want to take an express route from the first stages of learning straight to leadership. But of course, it doesn't work that way.

How does it work? **Leadership is not something you "do"; it is something that grows organically out of the natural rhythm of learning.**

When you start at the beginning of anything, you're at the highest level of anxiety. As you learn—through study and doing, information and experience, book smarts and street smarts—you gradually lower your level of anxiety by raising your level of mastery.

As you continue climbing that ladder of knowledge (remember, right foot–left foot, right foot–left foot, study–action, study–action) you keep your eyes on worthy mentors, always using learning through modeling as your learning gyroscope to keep you on track.

Using those three dimensions of learning—study, do, model—with Slight Edge persistence, in time your level of mastery rises to the point where you turn around and realize others are modeling you! You have become worthy of emulating. The cream has become butter; the hyacinth of knowledge has covered the pond of your effort. You have grown into leadership.

How do you become a leader? Through honestly pursuing the path of self-mastery and continuous learning.

Your Mastermind

Of all the books I have ever encountered in my pursuit of excellence as well as all the how-to's of success, Napoleon Hill's masterpiece *Think and Grow Rich*, which I have mentioned several times already, is the one of the most influential. When you ask successful people what factors most contributed to their success, this is the book they will most commonly cite.

During the twenty years it took Napoleon Hill to write *Think and Grow Rich*, he interviewed more than five hundred of the richest and most successful men and women in the world, and then painstakingly analyzed what he'd learned and spelled it out in the form of thirteen "success secrets." Many of those secrets have been woven throughout the Slight Edge principles, including having faith and a burning desire. We also already mentioned the "Mastermind" groups in Chapter 6 in order to inoculate yourself from the negativity (aka cuckoos). Here are a few more reasons Hill decided it was so important to create a "Mastermind" group.

"No two minds ever come together without thereby creating a third, invisible, intangible force, which may be likened to a third mind," wrote Hill. A group of like-minded, achievement-oriented individuals, he explained, could come together to create an association far greater than the sum of its parts, thus dramatically leveraging each other's success.

As two examples from startlingly different sides of the spectrum of human endeavor, he cites Henry Ford and Mahatma Gandhi as masters of the Mastermind principle, which he defines as: "The coordination of knowledge and effort of two or more people, who work toward a definite purpose, in the spirit of harmony."

Applying Hill's principle is simple: surround yourself with people of like mind and different talents and temperaments with the purpose of serving the goals of every member of the group. Associate with these people on a regular basis.

Remember that you're always dealing with gravity: one against nineteen, all the time. The ninety-five percent will always tend to be cynical, skeptical and negative; even when motivated by the best of intentions, they will attack you and bring you down.

Apply the Law of Association. Create your own Mastermind, a group of those who have chosen to live among the five percent, and let them support you, let them be the lift beneath the wings of your dreams.

KEY POINTS OF CHAPTER 10

The greatest gift you could ever give yourself is also the wisest business investment you could ever make. What is this mysterious gift? It is your own personal development. Invest in your own improvement, your own personal growth and betterment.

Investing in Personal Growth

The Slight Edge has been especially helpful in the area of personal development. I have always been around people who felt that it was a waste of time to sit and read books. Now, I take the time every day to read at least 10 pages, and in the past year I have read 15 books. The wealth of knowledge and ideas I have gained is priceless.

—*Jane Lehman, Lexington, MI*

I have always believed that having a great philosophy is the foundation for success. Although I was never an avid reader of books, primarily due to not realizing the proper skills of time management, it did not enter my mind to just read 10 pages per day. I'm now reading five books and feel like I'm moving in a direction that I never dreamed possible.

—*Peter Klochko, Northville, MI*

We have always believed personal development is an inner journey and you will not get there overnight, and that is one of the most important principles Jeff teaches in *The Slight Edge*. I learned the practical concept of "How do you eat an elephant?" One bite at a time, of course. That is what Jeff Olson taught me through his philosophy as I read *The Slight Edge*. No one changes overnight, and you are not going to absorb the full material in a good book overnight. By reading 10 pages of a good book everyday our concept of patience was re-enforced, our concept of self worth was re-enforced, our concept of commitment was re-enforced, by simply applying these principles, we are better people.

—*Ron Forrester & Leslie Hocker, Houston, TX*

I was introduced to the Slight Edge philosophy when I was 19. Before that time I never really saw myself doing much with my life. I couldn't hold conversations with strangers and I truly wasn't interested in people. I wouldn't say I was a troublemaker, but I was willing to settle for mediocre. I was an average student in high school and dropped out of college my first year. After reading the book, I wanted more. I started diving into other great books, reading 10 pages a day and I just started transforming. I wanted to be successful. I wanted to talk to other people about success. At every job I held, I shot straight up to management, ahead of people who had worked at the establishment for years. Even more importantly, successful people began being attracted to my attitude and my energy.

I'll never forget the day at the gym when a highly successful real estate developer approached me. He said he had a great location for a new business. He said if I was interested he would finance the entire project in the beginning and help me get the new company running until I could repay him through the cash flow of the business. The opportunity literally fell in my lap and I jumped on it. To this day the business is up and running successfully. We have conquered our first year of business and in a couple of years I will begin the expansion of my company. I'm 22 years old and if it wasn't for the Slight Edge principles, and investing in myself by reading 10 pages of a good book every day- I wouldn't be the man I am today.

—*James Fortner, New Haven, MO*

CHAPTER 11

Turning Your Dreams into Reality

> *Whatever you can do, or dream you can, begin it.*
> *Boldness has genius, power and magic in it.*
> — Johann Wolfgang von Goethe, *Faust*

There are entire books written about how to set, pursue and achieve your goals, and some of them are actually pretty good. You may or may not need an entire book; that's up to you. I like to keep things as *simple* as possible, because simple is usually far more effective—and most importantly, *simple* is what works best with the Slight Edge. Remember "easy to do," and you won't stray far from having your hands on the Slight Edge.

While everyone has a somewhat different approach to goal setting, there are four simple and fundamental steps you need to take for your dreams to turn into reality. Everyone who has ever created success, whether consciously or not, whether using this specific language or not, has gone through these four steps. They are the four universal truths of reaching for a big dream.

For a goal to come true:

You must write it down, make it specific and give it a deadline.
You must have a plan to start with.
You must understand and pay the price.
You must look at it every day;

STEP ONE: Write It Down

The most critical skill of achieving success in any area whatsoever, from sports to high finance, radiant health to fulfilling relationships, is the skill of *envisioning*. Envisioning something simply means having the ability to create a vivid picture of something that hasn't factually happened yet, and make that picture so vivid that it feels real.

Envisioning doesn't happen simply by creating a picture in your mind. If your dreams and aspirations are happening in your mind only, that's not envisioning, that's wishful thinking. It's like saying, "I'll give it a try"—which as Yoda pointed out, really doesn't cut it. ("Do or do not—there is no *try*.")

Envisioning means quite literally making something up out of thin air—and *making it real*. By definition, you can't do that within the confines of your skull. It needs to become physical; it needs to involve your senses. In other words, you need to write it down. Making pictures of it, which people sometimes call a "dream board," is even better. Speaking it out loud is the most powerful of all. But at the very least, write it down. The moment you do, it has started to become real.

What do you dream about? Pick a dream you have, any dream: your dream house, your dream car, dream vacation, dream job, dream marriage, dream career. Pick a dream that you'd really love to have come true. Write it on the first line below. Then pick another, and another, until you have five dreams.

If you're hesitating, know this: these dreams may be as huge or as small as you like; neither is "better" or more or less worthy to make real.

1. _____

2. _____

3. _____

4. _____

5. _____

Good. Now, let's have you add two descriptors that will make your dream more concrete: *what* and *when*.

First, go back to each dream and add whatever wording you need to make each dream absolutely specific. For example, if you had a dream to "be financially free," what does that mean, specifically? How much money do you need in the bank or investments, or coming in as annual income, to achieve what you call "financial freedom"? If there are any other conditions that need to be met (such as "being completely debt-free"), add those in, too.

What if one of your dreams is "radiant health." How would you make that specific? One way would be to describe exactly how you feel, what kinds of activities you engage in and what they feel like. Imagine reading your dream to someone you care about, and that person saying, "I'm not sure I quite grasp what you mean. Can you tell me exactly what you're shooting for?"

Now, the second descriptor: *when?* It's often been said, **"Goals are dreams with deadlines."** Let's reshape your dreams into goals by giving them deadlines. Go back through each dream and answer the question, "By when?"

You've probably heard of the Pareto Principle, known more popularly as "the 80/20 rule," which says that, for instance, twenty percent of the people in a sales force produce eighty percent of the results. (Vilfredo Pareto, an Italian economist who promulgated his theories around the turn of the twentieth century, actually arrived at his formula, which is a bit more complex than a simple 80/20 rule, to describe the tendency of wealth, innovation and initiative to concentrate in a self-selected elite, no matter what the external social or economic system. In other words, Pareto was really describing the success curve and failure curve—the two sides of the Slight Edge!)

Here is another application of Pareto's Law: eighty percent of everything you do tends to get done in the last twenty percent of the time available! If you don't create a concrete deadline, that last twenty percent never seems to arrive ... and you're always living in the eighty-percent time that says, "some day ... "

Write your dreams down; make them vivid and specific; give them a concrete timeline for realization; and you've taken a giant step toward making them real!

STEP TWO: Start with a Plan

This is the point where people are often thrown off track. It's easy to assume that you need to put together the plan that will get you there—in other words, the *right* plan. The plan that will work. No. The point is not to come up with the brilliant blueprint that will take you all the way to the finish line. The point is simply to come up with a plan that will get you *out of the starting gate.*

You have to start with a plan, but the plan you start with will not be the plan that gets you there. Just for emphasis, I'm going to say that once more:

You have to start with a plan, but the plan you start with will not be the plan that gets you there.

What? That makes no sense at all! If this plan isn't going to get me to my goal, why bother designing it? What's the point? Aren't I just fooling myself with a pointless plan?

Not at all. You need a plan to start with, the same way you need a penny to start with before anything can double. The way you took your first baby step. The way you furrowed your brows, pursed your lips and struggled to sound out the first sentence you read.

Would that penny have financed an empire? Of course not. Would that first step have won the Boston Marathon? Would that first sentence have earned you a master's degree in literature? No, and no, and no. But without that penny, without that first wobbling step, without that first stumbling sentence, your dream—no matter how deeply you wanted it—would never have materialized.

People make the mistake of thinking they need the perfect plan. There is no perfect plan. By definition, there can't be, *because a plan is not getting there—it's only your jumping-off point.*

And that's the reason you need a plan: if you have no plan, there will be no jumping off. In fact, if you put too much energy into the plan, and make it too perfect, you're more likely to squelch all the life, spontaneity, intuition and joy out of the doing of it.

Do the thing, and you shall have the power. Don't try to figure it out! If you want twice the success, double your rate of failure.

You start with a plan, then go through the process of continuous learning through both study and doing, adjusting all the time through the *kaizen* of plan, do, review and then adjust, like a rocket to the moon—off track ninety-seven percent of the time, your gyroscope feeding information to your dream computer to bring you back on track ... You need a first plan so you can get to your second plan, so you can get to your third plan, so you can get to your fourth plan.

Success is the progressive realization of a worthy ideal. Keep holding that as your philosophy, and you will generate the attitudes and actions you need to keep progressively realizing a better and better plan.

Your starting plan is not the plan that will ultimately get you there ... but you need it so you have a place to start.

In my profession, training is a huge part of what drives the business. Training is the great equalizer: because we work with such large numbers and such a sweeping diversity of people from all types of backgrounds and walks of life, we train, train and train some more.

It's not that there's all that much to learn. It's like learning to play the piano: there are only twelve notes, after all. But to learn it, you need to hear it, and play it, over and over. It's as vivid an illustration of Slight Edge success as I've ever seen.

At the same time, I have very little regard for trainings that tell you, "This is exactly how you have to do it," because the actual sequence of actions and events that works will be different for everyone, every time. You can train people in the concepts, in how to think and what kinds of actions have worked, but you can't blueprint the specific sequence, because circumstances are always different.

This is why you need to have a plan to start with—but you cannot start with the plan that will get you there. You have to start with the philosophy that will take you; with the right *philosophy*, you'll find the plan.

STEP THREE: Know and Pay the Price

Aha, there's the catch! I knew it! Here comes the big sacrifice ... so, what will I have to do? Throw away my television? Say goodbye to all fun and forgo all my favorite foods? Give up a kidney?

Chances are, it's not quite that dramatic. Like anything else, when it comes to goals, we tend to see things like they're on the big screen; but they're not. Though your dreams may be big (in fact, I hope they're huge!), remember that the steps you're taking to get there are ... what, huge? No: small. Tiny. Baby steps. Easy to do.

The price you pay works the same way. You don't have to pay for your million-dollar dream with a million-dollar personal check. You can pay for it ... well, with a penny a day. But you do need to understand what that penny is, and you do need to pay it. **Whatever the dream, whatever the goal, there's a price you'll need to pay, and that means giving up something.**

It may be something as simple as giving up a type of junk food you're attached to, for the sake of your health; or something as subtle as giving up your right to be right, or your habit of exerting control over conversation for the sake of a relationship. It may mean postponing certain purchases or acquisitions, often called "delayed gratification," or letting go of some pleasures for the sake of the pursuit of a longer-term aim.

At a certain point in my life, when I'd suffered some huge setbacks and lost everything I had, I came to a critical point of decision. I'd been an athlete all my life, and at this point I'd become part of a softball team. We were serious, and we got pretty good. Before long, we were traveling and winning tournaments all over the place.

Then, I hit a point where I knew I had to get my career back on track. It was time to pick up the pieces, regroup and move on. I also knew I couldn't do this without changing something: I had to pay a price. It was a difficult choice, but I walked away from our softball team. My friends couldn't believe it. "You're quitting?!" And I said, "Hey you guys, you're still my friends, I love you, but get another outfielder." I took that same time and invested it elsewhere.

I had to plant and cultivate in a different field.

Remember, there aren't many millionaires who bowl over 100. Why not? Because they left the bowling league behind to build their fortunes. "Is that too large a price to pay?" is a question only you can answer. **Remember this: whatever price you pay, there's a bigger price to pay for not doing it than the price for doing it. The price of neglect is much worse than the price of the discipline. It may take a few years to put your success on track—but it takes your entire life to fail.**

STEP FOUR: Look at It Every Day

The single most compelling reason for writing down your dreams is so you can look at them and read them every day. The reason you need to look at them every day is the same reason you need to keep yourself in the company of positive people: **you need to counteract the force of gravity—or to put a different name to it, the force of mediocrity.**

Remember, it's nineteen to one—and you need to constantly remind your brain where it is you're headed or you'll drift away. If you don't keep yourself constantly, repeatedly focused on your destination, you'll be like a rocket ship without a gyroscope: you'll simply drift off gradually into the outer space of failure, never even coming remotely close to reaching the moon.

Surround yourself with it, keep your awareness in your face, look at it every single day. Your brain is far more complex and powerful than the biggest computer in the world, and your own subconscious is by far the biggest distraction you have.

Remember how many times you heard the word "No" by the time you hit first grade? Over 40,000 times—while you'd heard the word "Yes" only 5,000 times. Your brain has recorded an eight-to-one preponderance of "No," which translates into, "You can't do it ... It will never work ... That's impossible ... Why even bother trying?" We all come at this business of success with an extraordinary baggage of negative conditioning.

And that's all right. You and I can't live our childhoods over again, but we don't need to in order to fulfill our dreams. What we can do—and do need to do—is *surround ourselves with our own Yes's*. Surround yourself with messages that tell you your dreams are real, your dreams are real, your dreams are real.

Having your dreams concretely spelled out, on paper, in the most vivid and specific terms possible, and with a very tangible, concrete timeline, provides you with an "environment of Yes!" for your goals, dreams and aspirations. And when that nineteen-to-one force of gravity starts leaking from our subconscious and says, "Yeah, but are they really?"—we need to respond, *Yes! Yes! Yes! Yes! Yes!*

Here is the amazing thing—and I've seen this happen so many times, yet it never ceases to fill me with awe: when you set your goals, life has a way of rearranging itself, a series of events starts in motion that you could never have predicted or planned, to get you there. If you just sit there and try to figure it out, it doesn't happen. But when you surround yourself with your goals, your subconscious brain goes to work on it—and if you have the right philosophy, the philosophy of the Slight Edge, then you will come up with the right actions and keep repeating those actions ... and a series of events will kick in, including circumstances you could never have dreamed of, that will take you to that goal.

To give you an example, here is the true story of how I built the largest sales and distribution forces in all of Germany for one of my past companies, which has since become one of the largest such organizations in all of Europe and one of the most successful in the history of that industry.

Anatomy of a Breakthrough: How I Built a German Sales Force

One Friday morning, I woke up and turned on the TV while I was getting dressed. On television, someone was talking about a business opportunity and franchise show in Albuquerque. I thought, *Hey, maybe I should be in that.* I called the people running the show, asked if they had an opening, they said, "Yeah," so I changed my plans for the day and spent the next eight or ten hours shopping around, buying things for my booth, and making little signs and packages to hand out.

The next morning I showed up at the franchise show and found my way to my little booth. I'd never done this before. I was surrounded by really nice, professional booths—and I stood in my stupid little homemade booth, trying to hand out my little brochures. Across from me, another person with a booth was blowing up balloons shaped like bears. There we were ... Bear Man and me.

All day long, people would come over to see the Bear Man's balloons and I would try to hand out my information, but nobody paid any attention to me. I had three hundred packages to give out and hoped to get names and phone numbers from maybe ten or twenty people—but I could not give my stuff away.

Finally, I found a line that worked. As one person walked past me to go see the Bear Man's balloons, I caught his eye and said, "Would you be interested in some great propaganda?" He stopped and laughed, and said, "Sure." I used that line for the entire weekend, gave out all three hundred packages and got about twenty names.

One of them happened to be a doctor named Shapiro. The next week, I called Dr. Shapiro; we had a pleasant conversation, but nothing happened as a result. I called him again, and kept calling him. After about a month and a half of following up with him, he came to meet with me, liked what he saw, and got involved with my business.

About this same time, I learned that our company was planning to open in Germany in about six months. I got my Mastermind group together and said, "Guys, this is it, we're going to open up Germany." They said, "How?" I had no idea how. The only thing I knew how to do was *double my rate of failure ... Do the thing and have the power.* We thought about it, and I decided what we needed to do was find Germans.

So at our meetings, we began teaching this amazing, sophisticated strategy we had developed: *Find Germans.*

Eventually somebody came up with the idea of dropping in on the local Mercedes dealership; someone else visited the local German club. One by one, ideas started to percolate.

About two weeks later, Dr. Shapiro showed up at a meeting and said, "Hey, I found a German." I asked him, "What do you mean?" He said, "I'm talking to my neighbor while he's mowing his lawn and I say, 'Hey by the way, Bob, do you know any Germans?' and he says, 'Well, yeah, I know a guy who lives in Germany,' and I say, '*Really?!*' "

I told Dr. Shapiro to send this German person all my information because I was planning to go over there in a few months. He said, "Hey, Jeff, aren't you speaking over in Miami in a few months?" Yes, I was. "Well, this guy's coming over to the US and I think he's going to be in Miami then, too!"

A few months later, I go to Miami and sure enough, this fellow comes up to me afterward and talks to me: his name is Vin, he's from Germany, and he gets quite excited about going back to Germany and helping us open up there in a few months.

Except after Vin flies back to Germany, three months go by—and the company doesn't open in Germany after all. We have to delay the opening by at least another three or four months.

So I call Vin and tell him, "Hey, we're open in England, why don't you go over to England and start working over there? You can get some practice, and then when Germany does open up, you'll already know the ropes and be really ready."

So Vin and his wife Birgitte go to England, rent a little flat and start working there.

Now, one day Vin and Birgitte are walking around England when they happen to stop to talk to a man who's painting a house. As they get talking, they ask him, "Hey, do you know anybody in Germany?" and he says, "Oh, yeah, I know this guy in Germany, he's really successful there."

Months later, when I finally get to Germany, I go from city to city, meeting with people in hotel lobby after hotel lobby—Hamburg, Düsseldorf, Cologne, Heidelberg, Munich, Frankfurt … I don't know a thing about Germany, and I don't speak a word of German. But Vin and the housepainter's friend go with me, side by side, the whole time translating and helping me out, showing me around. At first, I'll be speaking to a group, then Vin will translate, then I'll say something else, then he'll translate. But soon something odd starts happening: I'll say something—and then he takes off in rapid-fire German and talks for five minutes straight before coming up for air. He doesn't need me to say anything else; he's doing fine without me!

By the time I left Frankfurt, we had launched Germany—and today those two men are both multimillionaires, with sales forces in all of Europe.

Now, here's the question I want to ask you: how did I plan that?! Maybe it was like this:

One day, I was sitting on my bed, putting on my socks, and mumbling to myself, *Now how can I build a huge European sales force?* I thought about that for a while, then slapped my forehead and said, "I got it! All I need to do is turn on the TV, they'll probably be talking about a franchise show—

"And if I go to the franchise show, chances are really good that I'll be stuck in a corner with some guy called the Bear Man who'll take everyone's attention off me so I won't have any success handing out my little brochures, which will make me figure out that what I should say to people is something like, 'Hey, would you be interested in some propaganda?' and if I do that not only will I hand out all three hundred of my little packages but I'll also get about twenty names—

"And one of those names will be a doctor from Albuquerque who won't really be that interested at first, but even though it could take me, oh, about three weeks of calling him, maybe the doctor will finally show up when I'm teaching people about how to ask everyone if they know any Germans, and this doctor will ask his next-door neighbor one day while he's cutting his grass (and it's a good thing it won't be raining that day, because then this carefully laid plan won't work) if he happens to know any Germans—

"And he will! He'll know this one person who not only lives in Germany, but happens to be coming over to Miami at the same time I'm going over there, which will work really well—

"Because even though he'll go back to Germany all excited about opening up there, if this plan works just right then that won't happen because it'll turn out that the company isn't ready to open up in Germany yet after all and that'll be just perfect because then I'll tell this guy, 'Hey, why don't you go over to England instead for a few months?' which my guess is he'll probably go ahead and do, maybe even renting a flat with his wife.

"Which will be just perfect, just like I planned it, because one day when they're walking, they'll walk right past this house, which will be timed just right (because as luck would have it, it won't be raining on that day either!) so they'll stop and strike up a conversation with this housepainter, which is *perfect* because I will have trained them to ask, 'Hey, do you know any Germans?' so they'll ask that question and if this all goes just according to my plan then the housepainter won't even have to stop and think about it 'cause he'll just say, 'Yes, actually, I do know a fellow in Germany, and in fact he's quite a successful bloke over there,' and that'll be perfect too because when I do finally get over there to Hamburg, even though it will look like I don't have the slightest clue about what I am trying to accomplish in Germany, the truth is that this guy who met me in Miami (the franchise show doctor's next-door-neighbor's friend) and the successful guy in Germany (the guy that the Miami guy's neighborhood housepainter knows) will meet me in the hotel and travel with me as my translators and because they'll be translating for me they'll understand the business better than anyone else I talk to by the end of visit—

"And then maybe those two guys will go on to build the largest sales and marketing organization in Germany, and one of the largest in all of Europe.

"Yeah ... " and I nodded sagely. "That should work ... Good plan, Olson!"

And I finished putting on my socks and shoes.

Do you think that's how it happened? Of course not! Then how did it?

The truth is, *I started with a plan.* My plan was this: I told people to ask others, "Do you know any Germans?" That was it. That was the plan.

And you know, it worked. A simple plan—you could even say, it was so simple it looked stupid. But if you start with a plan, and you practice those simple daily disciplines ... one plan leads to the next plan, leads to the next plan—

Can you imagine how many times this ridiculously unlikely chain of events could have fallen apart? (Twice, an innocuous afternoon rain shower would have scuttled it!) Why didn't it? Because we started with a plan, and then allowed the Slight Edge to work.

Until one is committed there is always hesitancy, the chance to draw back, always ineffectiveness. Concerning all acts of initiative (and creation), there is one elementary truth, the ignorance of which kills countless ideas and splendid plans; that the moment one definitely commits oneself, then Providence moves too. All sorts of things occur to help one that would never otherwise have occurred. A whole stream of events issues from the decision, raising in one's favor all manner of unforeseen incidents and meetings and material assistance, which no man could have dreamt would have come his way.

I have learned a great respect for one of Goethe's couplets:

> *Whatever you can do, or dream you can, begin it.*
> *Boldness has genius, power and magic in it.*

—W. H. Murray, *The Second Himalayan Expedition*

A whole stream of events ... which no man could have dreamt would have come his way. That strikes me as a very good description of how our German sales force came into being.

Don't try to figure out the whole race. Just figure out where to put your foot for the starting line. Just start. The result looks incredibly complex, but it's not; it never is. It's always the simple little things that take you there.

Everything you do, every decision you make, is either building your dream or building someone else's dream. Every single thing you do is either leading you away *from* the masses—or leading you away *with* the masses! Every single thing you do is a Slight Edge decision.

Our strategy for opening Germany seemed so ridiculously simple. What made the difference was that we did it every day. Did we have success in Germany after one day, one week, even one month? Of course not. We had nothing ... just a few names. And suddenly one day, those few names had blanketed Europe with a financial empire.

Just like the water hyacinth.

KEY POINTS OF CHAPTER 11

They are the four universal truths of reaching for a big dream.
For a goal to come true:
- *You must write it down, make it specific and give it a deadline.*
- *You must have a plan to start with.*
- *You must understand and pay the price.*
- *You must look at it every day.*

After many years of working in the real estate industry, I woke up one morning and realized I couldn't do it anymore. I was almost 40 years old, and already in full burn out mode. I took a vacation to Montana to try to rejuvenate and fell in love with 'big sky country' as it is called by many. Everything about the mountains and rivers spoke to me, and I knew that this was where I was going to live someday. I went back to Texas, left the real estate industry and began my own business, rejuvenated by the dream of 'big sky country.' I dedicated myself to consistent daily actions and modeling myself after others who were successful.

I started dreaming big, real big. Real, real big. It was exciting. I thought about a ranch in Montana in the mountains, backing up to thousands of Forest Service acres with trees, rivers and streams running through the property. I would have horses, of course, and lots of room for all my friends and family to visit and enjoy. I would build a 'convention center' on the property so I could have retreats for women and hold family reunions there all right there at the 'ranch.' Of course the reality of my living conditions at the time of that dream was pretty stark in comparison, but I didn't pay attention to where I was at that time. Instead I focused 100 percent on where I was going to be in five to 10 years. I looked at my goals every day and envisioned myself attaining them.

For years I poured over floor plans for my dream home. And all through those years of planning and dreaming for the future, I kept working on my business steadily and with intensity.

Then, you guessed it. One day I was taking a Sunday afternoon drive to look at the aspen trees turning gold in the fall and literally drove up to my dream place. It was in the middle of the national forest, with lots of trees and a stream running beside it. And right on the fence post by the gate was a for sale by owner sign. I drove up the hill and knocked on the door, and as they say, 'the rest is history'. Within 30 days I had purchased a beautiful 80-acre property that looked exactly like what I have been envisioning for over 10 years! I spent a year renovating the house to get it exactly like all the pictures I had collected over the years.

A lot of my friends and family wondered how did she do it? I can tell you exactly how it was done: by applying the Slight Edge in every part of my life. From my beliefs, philosophies, actions, disciplines, every single day. I changed language from 'can't, maybe, don't know' to 'can, sure, I will figure it out.' I changed my thought pattern and when faced with disappointment or so-called failure I asked myself, "What did you learn? The Slight Edge philosophy is life altering and now I am passing it on. I am teaching my children and grandchildren the same principles so they can be as blessed as I have been.

I hope you dream big and go for your dreams with your whole heart. If you will consistently apply the Slight Edge in every decision you make you will realize them very soon.

—*Kathy Aaron, Helena, MT*

CHAPTER 12

Living the Slight Edge

Gentlemen, this is a football.

—Vince Lombardi

With these words, the legendary football coach would begin each new season of training, never taking anything for granted and always viewing each of his players as a blank slate, despite the fact that they were all seasoned pros. The first time Lombardi uttered this famous line, Green Bay Packer great Max McGee delivered his own immortal retort: "Uh, Coach, could you slow down a little? You're going too fast for us," and got a chuckle even from the unflappable Lombardi.

The contemporary business world has an expression for this mindset: "Assume nothing." The Zen Buddhists call it "beginner's mind." It's a mindset of humility and fresh inquiry, always looking for the most meaning and importance in the smallest things. I can't think of a better or more eloquent way of expressing it than, "Gentlemen, this is a football."

No matter how great your aspirations, how tall the dream and great the leap it means, the eternally repeating truth of the Slight Edge is that it is always built of small, simple steps. Easy to do—and just as easy not to do. Don't go too fast, and don't be too proud to stop, look at your life, and tell yourself, "This is a football."

To the coach, the football was the single step that begins the thousand-mile journey.

The football was Lombardi's penny.

Now it's time to find yours.

What one simple, single, easy-to-do activity can you do, day in and day out, that will have the greatest impact on your health; your personal development; your relationships; your finances; and your life itself?

In this next section, I'll ask you to walk yourself through these five areas of your life, one by one, to examine what they mean to you and where your dreams lie in each; and then lay out for yourself your dreams as goals (specific, vivid and with a timeline); the price you're willing to pay; a plan to start; and finally, one simple daily discipline that you will commit to doing each and every day from now on.

Go ahead, now, and take this stroll through your life; take a pencil as a walking stick.

The Slight Edge and Your Health

Tell me what you eat and I will tell you what you are.
— Jean Anthelme Brillat-Savarin

They say "the way to a man's heart is through his stomach." I don't know about that, but I do know this: that is the way to his destiny!

Health is one of the great riddles of existence. The foundational importance of everyday health is one of the most commonly known truths of human existence, and at the same time, it is also one of the most commonly and blatantly ignored. Everyone knows that "if you don't have your health, you have nothing." Our language is brimming over with related figures of speech:

At least you have your health.
You're only as old as you feel.
An ounce of prevention is worth a pound of cure.

Of the three "self-evident, inalienable rights" that ring from the American Declaration of Independence like a trumpet fanfare—"Life, Liberty and the pursuit of Happiness"—the first, without which the other two are irrelevant, is Life. And the most basic condition for the free, unencumbered experience of Life itself is health. There is nothing more basic than health—and there is no area of life where the Slight Edge is more vividly in operation, working either for you or against you.

That is perhaps your most important choice, day by day and hour by hour: whether to let your eating and physical activity build your fondest dreams—or dig your grave with your teeth. Hamlet wondered, "To be, or not to be?" You get to ask yourself that—and answer it—with every meal.

I always start with the area of health because when I'm in good physical shape I need less sleep, think more clearly, feel better about everything, and get more accomplished.

My simple daily discipline for my health is to exercise for at least half an hour.

When I started doing this, I have to admit, it didn't thrill me. That first day I went running was a real drag. I'd let myself go physically; it was harder than I'd expected it would be. That first day I ran for only about ten minutes; then over the next several weeks, I slowly worked my way up to my daily half hour. But even before that first week was over, I actually felt better than I had in months.

I usually say that the Slight Edge does not work quickly, but the truth is that often you'll get positive results fairly quickly. You may not achieve your ultimate goal in a week, a month or even a year or two, but you'll see the positive changes far sooner than you might expect. That's the way it was with my running.

I've said that successful people are willing to do those things unsuccessful people are not. And sometimes those things are uncomfortable. There is always a price you pay, and for me the price included my initial discomfort. But that price was quickly paid in full, and within weeks that discomfort faded. Now I'm uncomfortable when I *don't* run!

Another great example comes from *The Slight Edge* reader Amber Thiel of Seattle. Her friend adamantly recommended *The Slight Edge* to her. As she read the book, she knew why her friend had put the book into her hands, she was a living example of applying the Slight Edge principles toward health. Here is her story:

> *The principles in* The Slight Edge *exemplified the EXACT approach we were using to teach people how to get to their ideal health and weight. We focused on empowering people to make small decisions every day, taking the focus away from the scale and focusing on the journey instead. It's not the one unhealthy meal or one skipped workout that causes you to gain 25 pounds; it's the daily unhealthy decisions that add up over the course of a year or two that causes the 25 pounds.*
>
> *The same principle applies to release 25 pounds. It's not one or two healthy decisions, but the compounding effect of daily healthy decisions over a long period of time. Soon after reading* The Slight Edge, *we decided to launch our "home health seminars" into a business that now touches individuals and families all over the world in their health. The name for our company became The Healthy Edge, inspired by* The Slight Edge. *The foundation of The Healthy Edge is five daily goals that, when done consistently, transform people's health, attitude, esteem and weight.*

—Amber Thiel, Seattle, WA

Amber is in great company, along with the many doctors who have written in to us to explain how they have incorporated Slight Edge principles into the health regimen they recommend to their patients. Taking control of your health is just a few daily actions away.

Those Slight Edge actions that are easy to do, and easy not to do? Soon, thanks to the powers of momentum, completion and habit, they become far easier to do than not to do!

Take a few moments to work out your own Slight Edge plan for your health. You don't need to feel limited or constricted by this exercise; you can always change and modify what you write here. Use a pencil! But do yourself a favor: don't skip over this and read on to the next step. Actually take the time to fill out each section, at least with some solid ideas to start with. You can always add to it and refine it later. In fact, you'll have to! That's how the Slight Edge works: you're not supposed to get it perfect the first time.

My dreams for my health (specific, vivid and with a timeline):

_____

_____

_____

_____

_____

Price to pay:

_____

_____

_____

_____

Plan to start:

_____

_____

_____

_____

One simple daily discipline:

_____

_____

_____

_____

The Slight Edge and Your Personal Development

*You will become as small as your controlling desire,
or as great as your dominant aspiration.*

— James Allen, *As a Man Thinketh*

If you could wave a magic wand and have either a million dollars in the bank or a million-dollar mindset, which would you choose? I wouldn't hesitate for an instant: I'd rather be worth it than have it. Why? Because if I'm penniless but I have a million-dollar mindset, then it won't be long before I have the million dollars. But even if I don't have a million-dollar mindset, even with a cool million in the bank, it won't be long before I'm back to being penniless again!

Your income will never long exceed your own level of personal development. It may take a jump through happy circumstance or a lucky break—but if your own development does not quickly rise to meet that new level, it will quickly bounce back to the level where your personal development limits it, sure as if it were on a rubber band.

The same is true of your health; and of your relationships; and of your career; and of every aspect of your life. Over the long term, the limiting factor is never circumstance or fate; the limiting factor is always you. In the same way, and for the same reasons, the limitless scope of possibilities is also defined by one factor: you.

You already know of my passion for this area, and my number one Slight Edge recommendation. I teach everyone I work with to read at least ten pages of a powerful, life-transforming book each and every day. At the back of this book, I provide a list of some of my favorites; please add to it. Building your own personal self-improvement library may be the single most valuable and important investment (after your personal health) that you can make.

In addition to reading ten pages a day, I also teach people to listen to a self-improvement CD or audio download for at least fifteen minutes every day. The average person spends between 250 and 350 hours every year driving to and from this place and that. That's about forty minutes to an hour each and every day. If you spend that time listening to educational and self-improvement material, you'll have the equivalent of a Ph.D. on any subject you choose in just a few years. That's the Slight Edge.

When you're in your car, you can listen to music; but why build Kenney Chesney's dream (even though he is my favorite!) or Taylor Swift's dream when you could be building your own? Listen to Jim Rohn's audio programs; he's a master at helping you build *your* dreams. **Turn your car into**

a drive-time university! There are hundreds of powerful, masterful men and women to choose from. But you do have to make the choice.

I run with an iPod® and a headset, so I'm listening to audios while I run, which doubles my improvement. I travel quite a bit; when I do, I always pack my running shoes and iPod—so my Slight Edge half-hour run goes with me no matter where I travel.

Because I double my time by listening to audios while I run, I also get to work directly on my personal development. Like health, this is a fundamental area for me, and is so powerful that it influences everything else going on in my life. When I first added the iPod to my daily run (in those days it was a Walkman), I started noticing positive changes in every other area of my life within the first couple of months.

Is it easy to do? Easy not to do? And if you don't do it, what will happen today? But that simple error in judgment, compounded over time, will leave you a willing participant in the conspiracy of mediocrity that nibbles away at the hopes, dreams and aspirations of the ninety-five percent who live out their days under the curse of Thoreau's famous epitaph for humanity (from *Walden*): "The mass of men lead lives of quiet desperation."

Listening to audio CDs is an especially powerful Slight Edge tool because it can turn your "down time" into *up* time and double your productivity. You can drive to the store, or work or school; you can jog, roller-blade, bike or walk; sit on planes, stand in line, pedal, row, ski, stretch and lift weights—all the while feeding your mind through life-transforming information.

And when you spend this time listening to true masters of the skills you seek to learn, you are using the third and most powerful method of learning: learning by modeling a mentor.

Take a few moments to work out your own Slight Edge plan for your personal development. Again, you need not feel limited or constricted by this exercise; you can always change and modify what you write here. But don't skip on to the next step: do yourself a favor and put down some initial thoughts. Use a pencil!

My dreams for my personal development (specific, vivid and with a timeline):

_____

_____

_____

_____

_____

Price to pay:

_____

_____

_____

_____

_____

Plan to start:

_____

_____

_____

_____

_____

One simple daily discipline:

_____

_____

_____

_____

_____

The Slight Edge and Your Relationships

> *No man is an island, entire of itself; every man is a*
> *piece of the continent, a part of the main. If a clod be*
> *washed away by the sea, Europe is the less, as well as*
> *if promontory were, as well as if a manor of thy friend's*
> *or of thine own were. Any man's death diminishes me,*
> *because I am involved in mankind; and therefore never*
> *send to know for whom the bell tolls; it tolls for thee.*

— John Donne, *Devotions Upon Emergent Occasions*

One of the great ironic truths of human existence is that no matter how great our accomplishments, it is ultimately other people who give it meaning. One reason that *Citizen Kane* continues to rank among the greatest films ever made even today, more than sixty years after it was made, is that it makes such a powerful statement of this truth: despite all his larger-than-life accomplishments, his millions, his international power as king-maker and -breaker, in the final hour of his life, Charles Foster Kane was consumed by a single thought: anguish over being ripped from his childhood and thrust into the world alone at the age of eight. The "great man" had no one to share his conquests and accomplishments with.

Earlier in this chapter, I wrote that the importance of health is "one of the most commonly known truths of human existence—and also one of the most commonly and blatantly ignored." The same can be said for the importance of relationships. How often have you heard of a successful businessperson who achieved great financial success only at the expense of those two most precious assets, good health and a rich family life?

When writing about the Law of Associations, I mentioned the importance of who you associate with in terms of its strategic effect on you. But there is a greater truth about your associations, too, because the relationships you choose are not only a means to an end, they are also an end in themselves. All the success in the world, as Charles Foster Kane learned, means little if there is no one to share it with.

Relationships, too, are both built up and torn down in the subtlest ways. Because most people are not aware of the Slight Edge, the progress of their relationships tends to be a mystery. What makes a marriage grow richer over the years for one couple, and grow stale, empty and bitter for another? Nine times out of ten—or better, nineteen times out of twenty—there is no single, significant answer. It is the little things, day by day, that add up over time to unshakable happiness or unsalvageable misery.

You've no doubt heard the expression, "It's the little things that count." There could scarcely be a more succinct statement of the Slight Edge—and chances are, you've heard it said in the context of a relationship. The remembered birthdays, the little gifts, the gestures, the kind words, the remembered favorite color. The five minutes, snatched from an impossibly hectic day, to drop everything and hear the other's news. The word of encouragement; the reminder of your own belief in the other person. The listening.

It's been said that the most important statements of friendship are usually spoken with five words or less. That is the wisdom of the Slight Edge: those tiny thoughts and gestures that are startlingly easy to do ... and tragically easy not to do.

The future of every relationship you have, like that of your health, is a choice that is always in your hands, and it's no bigger than a penny. The key is to make the choice—and keep making it.

A special category of relationships, of course, is family. If you have children, you probably already know that they are in many ways your greatest legacy. No matter what the state of the educational system (and regardless of the decade or generation you're looking at, it always seems to be in a state of crisis!), the single most powerful influence on children will always be the people who raise them.

My daughter Amber has unusually high self-esteem. This is no accident; in fact, it is a blessing I owe to the Slight Edge. When Amber was little, my wife and I knew that no matter how much we might want to, we could not change the 40,000 "No's" she was going to experience. That's what parents do: we set boundaries. The "No's" are something we do to protect our kids. That's our job.

We couldn't change the number of "No's"—but we could change the number of "Yes's." And that is exactly what we did.

One of the greatest gifts you can give your children is more "Yes's." So every time we said "No," we found a way also to say "Yes." By the time Amber went to school, she brought with her some 40,000 "No's," but she also brought with her something to the tune of *160,000* "Yes's"—four times as many Yes's as No's. It changed her philosophy and her view of life. It changed her view of herself. As a result, it will change her entire life.

Though children are special, they are not unique in this respect: they are human beings, and so is everyone else. What kind of influence can you have on people simply by providing them with more "Yes's"? More influence than you can possibly imagine.

I want you to hear from Renee, Amber's mother and my best friend, because she consistently applies the Slight Edge to relationships better than anyone I have encountered:

> *My first Slight Edge experience began as a child watching my mother interact with everyone around her. She made a difference every day, with friends and strangers alike. We didn't know what it was at the time, but it was definitely the Slight Edge in action. I didn't inherit her gregarious personality, but I did inherit her heart for people.*
>
> *I have made it a habit to be present with whomever I happen to be with. To take an interest in them and what is going on in their world, to ask questions, and most important, to give encouragement for a job well done, to notice and comment on what is right, and not what is wrong. I do this even with strangers that I might possibly never see again, for sales clerks, wait staff, and people I come across during my daily activities.*
>
> *I don't know how this affects the people I encounter, except to know that so often people who are checking me out at the grocery store will spill their hearts and tell me so much of their personal lives, because for a moment, I took an interest in them.*

We never know what people may need at any given point, and a smile, a moment, a sincere question about their lives, someone to listen, might just be exactly what a person needs. It is one of those Slight Edge disciplines. It would be so easy not to talk to them, to be caught up in my own thoughts, to not have an interest outside of myself. But as this phenomenon called the Slight Edge catches on, what if we used it beyond ourselves, what if we used it to create a positive moment for all who cross our paths. It would eventually start to mess with the negativity and indifference that so often greets us.

I try to do the same but on a much bigger scale with my friends and family. Once my daughter was born, I felt as if I had begun the most important job of my lifetime. I have practiced the Slight Edge with her, in every way imaginable, with the best possible results. My encouraging, positive, you-can-do-anything attitude has been practiced more on her than on anyone else in my life, from the time she was born. (She is an only child, so no one got left out!)

With children it is often so much easier to take the path of least resistance, to let them eat that fast food they love rather than cook something healthy, to let them watch TV rather than read to them, to let them play video games rather than to interact with them. I worked to make the Slight Edge decision every day in every way with her, and it has paid off in a big way. She is now an adult, a woman who knows she can do anything she sets her mind to. I can't really list the ways it has paid off without sounding like a typical proud mother, but I think you can imagine the outcome!

I can no longer make the Slight Edge decisions for her, but the wonderful result is that now she is making her own Slight Edge decisions, and I am sure she will pass those on to her children.

Everything You Do Is Important

Toss a rock into a pond, and you'll see ripples from its impact spreading out until they reach the opposite shore. The same thing happens in life—only in most cases, you never see those ripples.

Everything you do is important. When you smile at a child and encourage him, or scold him and tell him he's no good—in either case, you may see the splash it makes, and you may see the first or second ripple, but the impact goes far, far beyond what you see. You don't see all the ripples.

You teach someone to read ten pages of a good book a day, and you may see how it changes her, but chances are you won't see how it changes her kids, and her kids' friends, and their friends. And as these ripples spread out, they grow bigger! For better or for worse, with positive impact or negative impact, even your smallest actions create a ripple effect that has an incalculably great impact on the world around you.

No doubt, you recognize this description of the "ripple effect"—it's our old friend, the Slight Edge.

Now, take a little time to think about the relationships in your life, and jot down a few thoughts about how you might work out your own Slight Edge plan for deepening, strengthening and enriching those relationships. This is perhaps the most personal area of the five, and if you feel safer (since someone else might later be reading this copy of *The Slight Edge*), copy the worksheet below into a diary or journal, and fill in your answers there. Either way, do take the time to give it some thought and come up with your own answers. This is your life; this is the reason you're reading this book.

My dreams for my relationships (specific, vivid and with a timeline):

_____

_____

_____

_____

_____

Price to pay:

_____

_____

_____

_____

Plan to start:

_____

_____

_____

_____

One simple daily discipline:

_____

_____

_____

_____

The Slight Edge and Your Finances

Winning is a habit. Unfortunately, so is losing.
—Vince Lombardi

It's no accident that our exploration of the Slight Edge began with the story of a penny doubled. The world of finance is one of the easiest places to see, objectively and logically, the power of the Slight Edge in action. Everyone knows about the power of compound interest, right?

Wrong. Everyone *thinks* they know about the power of compound interest; but most don't, not really. How many really do understand this power? Five percent ... the ones on the success curve side of the Slight Edge.

Remember the Pareto Principle as applied to your goals deadlines? "Eighty percent of everything you do tends to get done in the last twenty percent of the time available." There's a similar law at work in most people's finances, only it's worse. It's Parkinson's Law (coined by Prof. Cyril Northcote Parkinson): "Work expands to fill the time available for its completion." As applied to personal finances, it goes like this: *Whatever I have, I spend.* And for the last few generations, where easy-to-get consumer credit has flourished like weeds, it has come to be more like, *Whatever I have, I spend a little more!*

There is some good news here; recently , the common sense of Slight Edge personal finances has started making a comeback. The book *The Millionaire Next Door* bucked the trend toward flashier, Donald Trump–style how-to finance books and instead gave example after example of how a cross-section of extraordinarily ordinary people became wealthy—without inheritance, without high-paying jobs, without making a killing in the stock market, without any of the usual "breakthrough" paths to riches, but by doing simple, easy things every day.

The first of its seven rules was, "Always live below your means." The book became a runaway best-seller.

When Stanley and Danko's book came out, my friends started reading it and calling me up, one by one, and saying, "Hey, Jeff, I just read this book, and it's about you!" For years, I kept our family living on $4,000 a month, no matter how much my income increased, and I wouldn't let us raise that monthly threshold until I had a million dollars (after taxes) in the bank. Then I raised it to $5,000!

"Living below your means" is a classic Slight Edge strategy.

You know where I got this Slight Edge financial philosophy from? Someone very dear to me: my mom! My mom worked for the majority of her career at a

Methodist church. She worked hard and saved wisely. When she was nearing retirement we were discussing her future when she modestly told me that she had saved through the years and was retiring as a millionaire! I was floored! Here was a millionaire next door that I never even knew about!

David Bach's *The Automatic Millionaire*, continued in the same vein, and this book, along with his other titles (*Smart Women Finish Rich, Smart Couples Finish Rich* and *Start Late Finish Rich*), as well as his appearances on *The Oprah Winfrey Show*, have brought Bach's common sense, Slight Edge financial advice into millions of households.

I'll bet you already have some very concrete thoughts about this area! Perhaps you've even been working this part out in the back of your mind ever since you read the story of the wealthy man and his two sons. Now's the time to start putting some of your thoughts to paper, and sketch out an initial plan for realizing your financial dreams and goals.

My dreams for my finances (specific, vivid and with a timeline):

_____

_____

_____

_____

_____

Price to pay:

_____

_____

_____

_____

Plan to start:

_____

_____

_____

_____

_____

One simple daily discipline:

_____

_____

_____

_____

The Slight Edge and Your Life!

There are only two paths in life. While we are traversing them, and especially in the earlier stages of the journey, they can often look alike, because appearances can be deceiving (and almost always are!). But they lead ultimately to very different places. One path leads to regret; the other leads to fulfillment.

In a typical goal-setting workshop, participants are often asked to set goals for a year ahead, five years, even ten years ahead. I went to a seminar once that had a unique approach: we were asked to set *one-hundred-year goals!*

What kind of goal would you set for one hundred years from now? What kind of impact can you imagine yourself having on the world that will last long after your own life has run its course? What will people remember you for after you have come and gone?

What impact do you wish to have on the world?

I used to ask people to think about their careers, their social and community activities, and their spiritual lives as distinct, different areas, much like their health and finances. I've come to look at this a little differently; I have realized that I would rather ask a larger question that embraces all these—career, social impact and spiritual life—as well as many others:

What do I want my life to mean?

This is the biggest area of all, because it includes all the others. Don't let it's sheer size and scope intimidate you. After all, what we're looking for here is simple, little things you can do every day—things that are as easy to do, as they are not to do. The key is not to spend too much time on this. Do the thing, and you shall have the power. Go ahead: take a pencil in hand and sketch it out. Remember, it's your life; what would you like it to mean?

And remember this, too, no matter how lofty or long-term your life dreams may seem: "Gentlemen, this is a football." It starts with a penny. Start finding your pennies.

My dreams for my life (specific, vivid and with a timeline):

_____
_____
_____
_____

Price to pay:

_____
_____
_____
_____
_____

Plan to start:

_____
_____
_____
_____
_____

One simple daily discipline:

_____
_____
_____
_____

KEY POINTS OF CHAPTER 12

What one simple, single, easy-to-do activity can you do, day in and day out, that will have the greatest impact on your health; your personal development; your relationships; your finances; and your life itself?

Examine what they mean to you and where your dreams lie in each; and then lay out for yourself your dreams as goals (specific, vivid and with a timeline); the price you're willing to pay; a plan to start; and finally, one simple daily discipline that you will commit to doing each and every day from now on.

Usually, break-ups are considered by most as one of the most painful experiences a person can ever encounter. When my relationship of five years came to an end, I did some soul searching and relived every moment I realized that I had not shared my voice in my relationship and I did not want that pattern to continue. I became inspired by this time in my life and began to become the authentic total female package. So with complete *faith*, I made another *step, a decision*. I would share my insights with every woman I know because at the end of the day every woman is already, *The Total Female Package*, and has all of the answers she needs inside of her to live her best life.

My break-up turned out to be a blessing because my first solo book project, *The Total Female Package*, which is based on the 13 mirrors that every woman possesses, took form, and for the past two years I have been working on building the movement around its message.

I completed the manuscript over six months in a total of 40 hours. I broke up the days I would write so I didn't feel overwhelmed by the project in addition to my present commitments. I began to share it with everyone I knew, word of mouth, social media, emailing, and every bite-size chunk of action moving it forward helped. I started to receive calls asking me to speak at events and recently co-founded a women empowering women community to share the 13 mirrors, which has grown to six cities.

The mirrors have a life of their own now and I can honestly attribute it to taking small manageable steps along my journey. The key was in allowing the magic to come from taking action with Slight Edge moves daily and not getting discouraged. Right now, inside of you, you may have a really big dream and it may seem out of reach. When you break it into bite size chunks, manageable steps, anything is possible. One day with time, you will wake up in the midst of what seems like a quantum leap in your life but in reality is an idea or dream you nurtured by expressing your faith in action daily. The simple Slight Edge formula has made all the difference in achieving my goals and it can for you too if put into practice.

—*Novalena Betancourt, San Diego, CA*

CHAPTER 13

Where to Go from Here

Some day, when I have the time, I'm going to ... Some day, when I have the money, I'm going to ...

Have you ever said that? "Some day ... " It's a way we have of reinforcing the illusion that the future is safely far removed, that it doesn't really touch us. It's a lie. Not an intentional, willful deception, but a lie nonetheless.

Let's say that, "some day," I'm going to travel around the world. If that's really true, if I absolutely intend for that to happen, then I'm making plans. If it's not practical today for me to just up and circumnavigate, I can look at what needs to happen first, and second, and third, to end up with that result.

When I set that process in motion, the words "some day ... " disappear. I'm making it happen today, right now. *In a very real sense, I am* already *taking the trip. It may be three years before we actually take the trip, but the words "some day ... " no longer apply, so I stop using them.*

When I say "some day ... " I'm not really talking about the future. The future is a reality that I'm connected to by what I'm doing right now. "Some day ... " is about some vague possibility that I'm not taking seriously.

"Some day ... " is not a vision of my future. "Some day ... " is a fantasy— nothing more.

Here's the damage we do with this illusion. We give weight to our "some day ... " fantasies; we squeeze some sense of enjoyment from them as if they were real—and thereby give ourselves permission to take no practical action whatsoever while we swim in the comforting sense that those some-day scenarios will move closer to the unfolding present on their own.

They won't. The wistful, wouldn't-it-be-nice pretendings of maybe-futures do not insert themselves into your reality of their own accord. You've got to go claim them. Ask yourself: "What is there in my life that I hold as 'Some day ... '?"

Some day ... The eighth day of the week. The only day that never comes. This is the day—this one. Right here. Right now.

— John David Mann, *The Eighth Day of the Week*

Abraham Lincoln spoke about taking twice as long to sharpen the axe as to hack at the tree. In your life, you are the axe; the Slight Edge is how you sharpen it. Sharpen yourself and pursue your path through those simple, small, easy disciplines, and compounded over time, they will take you to the top.

Do one simple, daily discipline in each of these five key areas of your life— your health, your personal development, your relationships (which includes family), your finances, and your life overall (which includes the meaning and purpose of your life)—that forwards your success in each of those areas ...

Make a habit of doing some sort of daily review of these Slight Edge activities, either through keeping a journal, a list, working with a Slight Edge buddy, a coach, or some other regular, consistent means ...

Spend high-quality time with men and women who have achieved goals and dreams similar to yours; in other words, model successful mentors, teachers, gurus, masters and allies, and do it daily, weekly and monthly ...

... and you will find yourself on the success curve—and you *will* turn your dreams into realities.

Successful people do what unsuccessful people are not willing to do; they put the Slight Edge to work for them, rather than against them, every day. They refuse to let themselves be swayed by their feelings, moods or attitudes; they rule their lives by their philosophies, and do what it takes to get the job done, whether they feel like it or not.

Successful people don't look for shortcuts, nor do they hope for the "big breakthrough." They are always open to quantum leaps, knowing that such opportune moments do present themselves from time to time, but they focus on sticking to their knitting and doing what they've put in front of themselves to do. They step onto the path of mastery and once having set foot there, they stay on that path throughout their lives.

Successful people never blame circumstances or other people; instead, they take full responsibility for their lives. They use the past as a lesson but do not dwell in it, and instead, let themselves be pulled up and forward by the compelling force of the future. They know that the path that leads to the success curve and the one that leads to the failure curve are only a hair's breadth apart, separated only by the distinction of simple, "insignificant" actions that are just as easy not to do as they are to do—and that this difference will ultimately make all the difference.

Successful people know how to use the natural tension to close the gap from point A, where they are, to point B, where they want to be. They understand why the tortoise won the race; they know that "steady wins the race," and that the Slight Edge is the optimal rate of growth for them.

Successful people practice the daily disciplines that are assured to take them to their final destination. They show up consistently with a good attitude over a long period of time, with faith and a burning desire. They are willing to pay the price and practice Slight Edge integrity.

Successful people focus on having a positive outlook, but understand that the funk get's everyone—and when it comes for them they embrace it, knowing it is just refining them. They take baby steps out of the funk—and step back into positivity.

Successful people use inertia to build momentum, making their upward journey of success easier and easier. They know how to identify habits that don't serve them and replace them with those that do. They understand the powers of reflection, completion and celebration and they harness them constantly, using their radar for unfinished business to propel them forward rather than being sucked backward and downward.

Successful people acquire the three kinds of knowledge they need to succeed. They create an ongoing support system of both book smarts and street smarts, learning through study and through doing, and they catalyze and accelerate that knowledge by finding mentors and modeling their successful behavior. They plan, they do, and then they review, again and again and again.

Successful people are always asking: "Who am I spending time with? Are they the people who best represent where I want to be headed?" They form powerful relationships with positive people; they carefully build Mastermind groups, work with those groups regularly and take them seriously; and they do not hesitate to disassociate themselves, when necessary, from people who are consistently negative and threaten to drag them down.

Successful people read at least ten pages of a powerful, life-transforming book each day, and listen to at least fifteen minutes of educational and inspirational information every day.

Successful people go to work on their philosophy first, because they know it is the source of their attitudes, actions, results and the quality of their lives.

They understand that they can increase their success by *doubling their rate of failure*.

They understand activity and because they *do the thing*, they *have the power*.

They understand the power of simple things.

They understand the power of daily disciplines.

They understand the power of the water hyacinth, and know how to use it.

They know how to keep paddling when others give up and sink.

They know when they are being offered the choice of wisdom.

Successful people understand the Slight Edge, and they put it to work for them.

So ... where do you go from here? Find your penny—then start doubling it.

Afterword:
The Slight Edge Next Generation

Individually taking responsibility, collectively changing the world.

by Amber Olson

If there is one thing that is clear about the Slight Edge philosophy, it is this: the longer you make positive choices every day, the more success will accumulate in front of you. That is precisely why I love talking about the Slight Edge philosophy with the Next Generation (which I consider anyone in their teenage years all the way through their late twenties, because the most abundant resource available to them is *time)*.

Through my parents and others, I have seen the impact of a lifetime full of right and wrong decisions and where they lead you. I am forever grateful to have had the Slight Edge philosophy instilled in me at a young age, because I was able to end up on the positive side of the Slight Edge curve by being aware that the choices I make on a daily basis matter.

On the other hand, as I approach my first high school reunion, it saddens me to see where some of my high school acquaintances have ended up. These were people who had everything in place. They were popular, outgoing, had loving families, yet somehow never realized that the Slight Edge was working against them. The small errors in judgment repeated daily over time landed them far from where they wanted to be.

It is my deepest desire for the Next Generation of Americans to grasp the Slight Edge philosophy and to become true champions of it in their lives and in the lives of those around them. I truly believe the only way our country will truly flourish is if the Next Generation takes responsibility for their lives. Only then can we collectively change the world.

We see more and more young adults and teenagers contributing to society and becoming champions for change. Charitable organizations founded by young adults are on the rise, as well as the amount of time they are contributing to serve others. Young adults are now heading up many environmental awareness efforts. I think it's safe to say that most of the Next Generation understand the problems that face our nation more than our politicians do. They know that the status quo isn't an option, and that we can't keep doing what we are doing and expect it to go away.

So how is the Next Generation going to change the world?

Beyond the fabulous humanitarian and charitable efforts they are contributing, **the Next Generation is going to change the world one individual at a time, one choice at a time, one day at a time.**

They are going to take responsibility for the lives they lead and leave the blame game to generations past. They are not going to look to the government to provide for their financial security—they will! They are going to be conscious about their health and vitality by treating their bodies like the precious gifts they are. They will value the biggest resource they have—*time*, and will make correct daily decisions that will improve every facet of their lives and are the key to long-term gains. How do I know this? Because they are already telling us so!

I have had the pleasure of working with and mentoring many teenagers, specifically on Slight Edge principles. Every time I facilitate a workshop with them, they share amazing stories with me that demonstrate their commitment to help themselves and their communities rise above current circumstances. They carry a message of hope and determination that is inspiring. The world they have been handed is not ideal to say the least, but they are making the best of their situation, and I'm confident that collectively they will move mountains.

Change Through Personal Responsibility

First, I want to paint an accurate picture of the times we find ourselves in, and then hopefully provide some useful steps that we can all follow to help bring *big change* through *personal responsibility*.

I have chosen to focus mainly on health and finances, as they are both issues that are at the forefront right now due to the down economy and the exploding obesity epidemic. These are areas that with some Slight Edge efforts can yield incredible results.

Health Check-in

Consider these sobering statistics:

• The prevalence of obesity has more than doubled in the last 20 years. The rate of adolescent obesity has tripled from 5% to 17%.

• Obese individuals (BMI 30+) account for 1/3 of the U.S. population. And overweight individuals (BMI 25-29) account for another 1/3 of the population.

• Obesity can lead to coronary disease, type 2 diabetes, high blood pressure, breathing problems, and an increased risk of many degenerative diseases.

• 70% of obese patients have had at least one cardiovascular disease risk factor due to excess weight.

• Unhealthy weight gain due to poor diet and lack of exercise is responsible for 300,000 deaths per year.

• The annual cost to society for obesity is $100 billion.

I think we can all agree that the majority of Americans are finally waking up to the concerns that the rapid rise in obesity is causing, due to the array of health risks it poses and the deaths related to it each year. So there is a cure: our daily choices!

Most Americans gain a few pounds a year and rarely notice. Does anyone else smell the Slight Edge here? But those few pounds a year are what is leading to the explosion in the growth of obesity, which translates directly to the related ailments type 2 diabetes, heart disease, high blood pressure and arthritis.

James Hill, director of the University of Colorado Center for Human Nutrition said, " If we could simply stop the weight gain, the public health impact we would see would be enormous."

The size of portions has greatly increased from 20 years ago. Take a look at the diagram of calories for 2 slices of pizza.

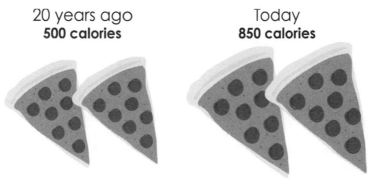

20 years ago
500 calories

Today
850 calories

That is an increase of 350 calories from 20 years ago. If you eat that extra 350 calories just two times a month, that would put on two extra pounds a year, or 40 pounds in the next two decades. And what if you are eating that extra 350 calories two times a month—where is that getting you? If you were to intake those 350 extra calories twice a week, that is 1,500 extra calories a month, which may not seem like much. But the compound effect of those extra calories over a year or years equates to many extra pounds. If that is not the Slight Edge working against you, I don't know what is.

Our portions are growing and growing, and we have rapidly become, pardon the pun, a "Biggie Size" nation. Meanwhile our daily activity is decreasing as we become more and more of a sedentary society. In fact, a very small percentage of the U.S. population have physically active occupations. And to make it worse, most are content to sit in front of the TV. Studies show the typical American spends 30 hours a week in front of the TV, yet only 27% of American get the recommended amount of weekly exercise. It seems we have some hours we can take from TV watching to re-invest in our health.

If we could dedicate 30 minutes a day to physical activity, we would see vast health benefits that no TV program can provide for us.

With just 30 minutes of physical activity a day you can:

• Reduce health risks (high blood pressure, stroke, osteoporosis, coronary disease, type 2 diabetes, certain cancers)

• Keep off excess weight

• Ward of viral illnesses

• Help keep your arteries clear

• Strengthen your heart

Research by Gallup Management concludes that "People who exercise at least two days a week are happier and have significantly less stress. In addition, these benefits increase with more frequent exercise. We found that each additional day of working out increased energy levels."

Wow! Can you see what big benefits are in store for you when you combine daily actions with a little discipline? Just start somewhere. It can be as easy as running a lap around your block. But if you don't start somewhere you will never attain your health goals.

Take the example of Jereme, 21, who discovered how small actions that compound over time make a difference. She has a passion for the sport of gymnastics. But the older she got, the more competitive the sport got.

Through the sport of gymnastics I have learned time management, self-discipline, teamwork, and most importantly the power of one's mind.

Gymnastics is a sport where progress is slow, skills are perfected through muscle memory, patience, and hard work. It is a very strenuous sport, both physically and mentally, and takes years of a solid foundation to build off of and improve. I did not have a solid foundation when I started competitive gymnastics at age seven. I had moved gyms two years after I started the sport and when I made the transition to the new gym, I basically had to learn the sport all over again. Through patience, hard work, and many hours at practice I became one the top ranked gymnasts in California. By age 12 I was practicing twenty five hours a week, and commuting two hours a day. There were days when my body hurt, when I had homework to do, when I thought I could not handle doing another routine at practice, when my mind and body wanted to throw in the towel and give. But I didn't. I learned through thirteen years of competitive gymnastics that there are going to be rough days, there are going to be days when you have given your full effort and you still come up short, there are going to be days that you want to forget. But in reality those are the days that make you stronger, that make you realize anything is possible with effort and a positive attitude. I learned at a very young age that your mind can control your body in positive and negative ways. Your thoughts are so powerful that they can pull you out of a rut or keep you buried deep within. Gymnastics is all about seeing and believing the positive. If you cannot see yourself succeed and improve, than there is no way that you will. Gymnastics has taught me that you cannot go through the motions, you cannot mark your skills. This concept can be brought over to daily activities in life. If you go through the motions of life without being conscience, without being purposeful, then it is a danger to you and others.

Small steps can make a huge difference, and with a strong support system, such as my teammates and family, good role models, and strong work ethic, barriers can be broken and huge accomplishments achieved.

Jereme is attending Oregon State University and was a part of the Oregon State Gymnastics Team for two years before a career ending injury forced her to retire from the sport. She continues to impart her wisdom to younger gymnasts, however, as a team coach at a private gym. Some of her students have competed at top state levels while simultaneously cultivating the same valuable life disciplines that Jereme first honed within gymnastics herself.

Great job, Jereme! Small actions compound over time. That means they grow in size and impact and lead to much bigger things. This is one of the most important lessons of the Slight Edge.

I had a friend who was trying to lose weight and loved the popular show *The Biggest Loser*. She got many great diet and exercise tips from the program. One day while she was watching she asked herself, *Why don't I jump on the elliptical machine while I watch this program? That way, after an hour goes by, I'm able to watch the show as well as get my daily exercise in.*

What a great way to customize her daily activity! Do what consistently works for you, but do something each day!

Believe it or not, maintaining vibrant health doesn't have to be complicated. Fad diets will always come and go. But at the end of the day it always comes down to your daily decisions.

Next Generation Health Plan

Here are some tips for optimal health:

- Be mindful of controlling your food portions.
- Eat slowly, paying attention to when you are full.
- Make good daily food selections (limit fatty foods and carbs, increase vegetables, healthy grains and lean proteins).
- Commit to 30 minutes of daily activity.
- Take daily vitamins to supplement your diet.

Financial Check-in

Let's start this section off with some more stunning statistics:

- Average household credit card debt is close to $16,000.
- Total bankruptcy filings in 2009 were 1.4 million.
- Total U.S. consumer debt is $242 trillion.
- 36% of people polled didn't know the interest rate on their credit card.
- Over a lifetime the average American pays over $600,000 in interest.
- 43% of American workers have less than $10,000 in savings.
- Only 16% of Americans feel confident in their ability to save enough for a comfortable retirement.

As our country deals with its own $13 trillion national debt and a shrinking Social Security system that is going bankrupt, it's pretty clear my generation will have no other choice but to take responsibility for our own savings and retirement plans. The good news is with proper planning rooted in the Slight Edge philosophy, we can rest assured we have everything we need to live out our golden years.

When it comes to finance you always want the Slight Edge of interest working *for you* not against you. If you understand the value of time and the amazing principle of compounding interest, then you know that consistently saving a little, especially at a young age, can help you amass a small fortune for your retirement.

For example, a 24-year-old invests $2,000 a year for six years. If left untouched in an interest-accumulating account, that $12,000 investment will be worth over a million dollars by age 65. That is an example of what we call the Slight Edge working for you. Unfortunately, interest can also have an opposite effect. This is how the Slight Edge can work against you. Say at age 24, instead of investing $2,000 a year for six years you purchased $2,000 worth of items on a credit card that you were not able to pay off at the end of the month. A latte here a DVD there, doesn't seem like much at the time of purchase, but when using a credit card to buy these items it can have a painful effect for years to come.

Let me show you.

If you added $2,000 worth of debt to your credit cards each year for six years and were never able to pay them down, that same interest that was working for you in the first example to become a millionaire is now working against you as your credit card debt accumulates compounding interest. That overspending of a few thousand dollars for a few years will be over $1 million in debt by the age of 65.

This is an extreme example, but I think you get the point. You have a choice with every dollar you earn. Are you going to put it somewhere where interest is working for you or against you? It's a Slight Edge decision you face every day.

Just for fun, let's break that $2,000 a year into a daily amount, since we are talking about daily disciplines here. That $2,000 a year is approximately $5.50 a day. I can easily save $5.50 a day, but the problem is it's just as easy not to save $5.50 a day because we don't recognize in that daily decision how much of our future financial security is resting on that $5.50 a day. I could easily spend this amount on a magazine, a large latte, a smoothie, etc. But knowing the Slight Edge like I do, I would know that saving $5.50 a day is going to get me to my $2,000 a year, which is eventually going to make me a millionaire at retirement.

I also know that putting $5.50 a day on a credit card I am not fully paying off will get me to my $2,000 a year of interest-bearing debt that is eventually going to sink me.

This is the reason so many Americans are swimming in credit card debt and facing bankruptcy. Not because of one bad financial decision, but because of several daily $5.50 bad decisions that have snuck up on them before they could even see what hit them.

So what is worth more to you, your $5.50 a day in magazines, lattes or video games, or knowing you are creating financial security for years to come? The choice is always yours, and you are always making it, so you better be aware of it.

I think *People* magazine put it best when they said, "A latte spurned is a fortune earned." I encourage you to figure out what financial guru David Bach calls your Latte Factor—what you are spending money on daily that isn't completely necessary. Know that the instant gratification of your purchase isn't worth the agony and frustration the compounded effect of these decisions will be. The Slight Edge decision to save that money and let the interest work for you will reap huge benefits for years to come. Invest a latte a day in your life and you will greatly rewarded.

Financial Tips for the Next Generation

- Determine your "Latte Factor" and make daily savings goals. Invest that money in a high-interest savings account or CD.

- Don't spend more money than you can pay off each month on your credit cards.

- Make sure you have the most competitive interest rates on your credit card. Be aware if you miss or are late on one credit card payment, your interest rate can greatly increase, sometimes even double.

- Meet with a financial mentor to determine the best way to save for college and retirement, and trace that back to daily goals.

Health and finances are just two main areas you can see the Slight Edge play itself out.

The main point I am trying to make is that the Next Generation has to be responsible for the outcome of their lives. Commit to being responsible for the trajectory of your health and finances. Commit to being responsible for you're your contribution to society. Ask yourself, "How do I contribute to preserving the earth's resources? How should I best give of my talents and time to help my community and help those in need?" Commit to being responsible for your education and career development. Teachers and parents are not ultimately who will decide if you reach your aspirations or attain your dream jobs—you will be!

Read how Slight Edge reader Alex Cross took responsibility for his own development.

> *I was having a hard time staying focused in my studies and was struggling to keep up. I was failing in half the classes I was taking and was slowly adopting a bad attitude toward school in general. At the urging of my dad I started to read at least 10 pages of a good book a day. I started with SUCCESS for Teens: Real Teens Talk About Using the Slight Edge. I started implementing daily study habits into my schedule and took small steps to improve my academic success.*
>
> *My grades improved to the rank of AB honor roll. At the end of the school year I received an award for "most improved student." The next year I continued the regimen of ten pages a night. That year I received a letter of commendation from President Obama for scholastic achievement and have been on AB honor roll ever since. I even recently received a commendation from Duke University for testing in the top 5% in the nation in a standardized test.*

No matter where are in life, high school, college, our first job, or building our careers we can all learn a lesson from Alex and commit to being the driver of our own development and our ultimate destiny.

There are numerous other areas of our lives where the daily decisions we make either move us closer or further away from our goals. What else is important to you? What else pulls at your heart? If it is environmental consciousness, trace back your carbon footprint on the earth to daily activities. If it is excellence in a sport, trace back the success in that sport to your daily activities. If it is academic excellence, trace back your end goal to your daily activities. The important part is to stay committed to what is important to you and stay committed every day. In a society that has a lack of commitment, we change channels, cell phones, jobs, even significant others at an alarming rate. Wouldn't it be refreshing if a generation was so sure of what they wanted and so committed to their cause they practiced unshakable commitment? I desire from the bottom of my heart to see this happen and I hope you will join me in living that out.

I believe the future is truly your canvas, where every possibility is available to you if you will only harness everything you need to make your goals and aspirations a reality. Be a generation of change. Be a generation of responsibility. Be a generation of discipline. Be a generation of commitment. Be a generation of the Slight Edge.

If you are a part of the Next Generation, I hope you choose the life of your dreams every day. If you are the parent, grandparent, uncle, aunt or teacher of the Next Generation, I hope you will help support and spread the Slight Edge Next Generation message.

Visit slightedge.org to learn more about how you can get involved in advancing the Slight Edge Next Generation message, as well as view additional resources and join a community of people dedicated to the Next Generation.

A Special Invitation

Be the change you wish to see in the world.
— Gandhi

We talked about the ripple effect earlier in the book. The ripple effect is so much bigger than the individual ripples we create. The magic lies in the collective ripple we make together in our community, our nation and the world.

We have created an online Slight Edge community to help you start your own positive ripples. The community was designed with you in mind—combining all of the best Slight Edge principles. You will have access to life-enhancing information and resources to help you stay on track with your daily habits. You will also experience the power of associations by being a part of a positive community with like-minded individuals. You will be able to interact and touch the lives of others as well as share your own Slight Edge story.

The Slight Edge could end here for you and you can move on with the rest of your life. Or you can be a part of a movement—a movement of things that are easy to do, easy not to do, yet make all the difference in the world.

This is a Slight Edge decision and I hope you make the right one!

It is my deepest desire that you leave a legacy of positive ripples.

Sincerely,
Jeff Olson

To join the Slight Edge community visit www.SlightEdge.org. You can also follow us on Facebook and Twitter. I look forward to seeing you there!

www.facebook.com/yourslightedge

www.twitter.com/yourslightedge

Life-Transforming Resources

The Happiness Advantage, Shawn Achor

As a Man Thinketh, James Allen

Multiple Streams of Income, Robert G. Allen

Smart Women Finish Rich, David Bach

The Automatic Millionaire, David Bach

Start Late, Finish Rich, David Bach

Start Over, Finish Rich, David Bach

Debt Free For Life, David Bach

The One Minute Manager, Ken Blanchard and Spencer Johnson

Mach II with Your Hair on Fire, Richard B. Brooke

The Aladdin Factor, Jack Canfield and Mark Victor Hansen

Dare to Win, Jack Canfield and Mark Victor Hansen

How to Win Friends and Influence People, Dale Carnegie

Acres of Diamonds, Russell H. Conwell

The Richest Man in Babylon, George S. Clason

The 7 Habits of Highly Effective People, Stephen R. Covey

The 8th Habit: From Effectiveness to Greatness, Stephen R. Covey

Outliers, Malcolm Gladwell

The Compound Effect, Darren Hardy

Delivering Happiness, Tony Hsieh

Think and Grow Rich, Napoleon Hill

Delivering Happiness, Tony Hsieh

Rich Dad Poor Dad, Robert T. Kiyosaki and Sharon L. Lechter

Cashflow Quadrant: Rich Dad's Guide to Financial Freedom, Robert T. Kiyosaki and Sharon L. Lechter

Conversations with Millionaires, Mike Litman, Jason Oman, et al.

The Greatest Salesman in the World, Og Mandino

The 21 Irrefutable Laws of Leadership, John C. Maxwell

Failing Forward, John C. Maxwell

The Power of Positive Thinking, Norman Vincent Peale

You Can If You Think You Can, Dr. Norman Vincent Peale

You Were Born Rich, Bob Proctor

Leadership Secrets of Attila the Hun, Wess Roberts

Cultivating an Unshakable Character, Jim Rohn

Seven Strategies for Wealth and Happiness, Jim Rohn

The Art of Exceptional Living, Jim Rohn

The Challenge to Succeed, Jim Rohn

The Five Major Pieces to the Life Puzzle, Jim Rohn

The Seasons of Life, Jim Rohn

The Happiness Project, Gretchen Rubin

True Leadership, Jan Ruhe, Art Burleigh, et al.

The Magic of Thinking Big, David Schwartz

Little Things Matter, Todd Smith

The Millionaire Next Door, Thomas J. Stanley and William D. Danko

21 Success Secrets of Self-Made Millionaires, Brian Tracy

The Science of Getting Rich, Wallace D. Wattles

All You Can Is All You Can Do, But All You Can Do Is Enough, Art Williams

Breaking the Rules, Kurt Wright

SUCCESS magazine

SUCCESS.com

SUCCESS for Teens, by the Editors of the SUCCESS Foundation

Visit www.SUCCESS.com to purchase many of these books and audio and digital download resources.

About the Author

JEFF OLSON has spoken to more than a thousand audiences throughout the United States and around the world. Over the past twenty years, he has helped hundreds of thousands of individuals achieve better levels of financial freedom and personal excellence.

Born and raised in Albuquerque, New Mexico, Jeff earned his undergraduate degree in marketing from the University of New Mexico, graduating at the top of his class. While in graduate school, he was hired by the Albuquerque Airport as one of the youngest airport managers in the industry. He then went to work for Texas Instruments (TI), where he worked his way through its sales ranks to become an intelligence systems manager in less than five years. He left TI to form Sun Aire of America, a company devoted to all aspects of solar energy, from design and manufacturing to marketing and distribution. Through all of this Jeff acquired exhaustive "street smarts" and formal business training in every aspect of sales, marketing and distribution, and within four years Sun Aire was one of the largest solar companies in the United States.

Since his experiences with TI and Sun Aire, Jeff has worked with a series of sales, marketing and distribution companies, building three different sales and distribution forces from scratch to multimillion-dollar organizations, one of which he was appointed CEO of. In the early '90s, he put in place a national satellite-training program for an independent sales force by placing 30,000 individual satellite dishes in homes across the country. Based on that experience, he went on to found TPN, The People's Network, a company that became one of the largest personal-development training companies in the nation. As the CEO of TPN Jeff was considered a thought-leader on the future of personal development, discussing the topic with the likes of Oprah, CEO of Simon & Schuster Dick Snyder, legendary producer Jimmy Bowen and many others.

Jeff has worked with such *New York Times* best-selling authors and legendary figures of personal development as Tony Alessandra, Les Brown, Nido Qubein, Jim Rohn, Brian Tracy and many others, producing more than 900 television programs with them and presenting seminars in every major city in the United States. He has been featured on the cover of *The Wall Street Journal* as well as other publications, including *Entrepreneur* and *SUCCESS* magazine.

Jeff contributed the Slight Edge principles to partner with the SUCCESS Foundation to create the book *SUCCESS for Teens: Real Teens Discuss Living the Slight Edge*, which has been distributed to almost two million teenagers.

Jeff describes himself as "a perpetual student of personal development," and he is as devoted to health and fitness as he is to personal and financial success. Jeff currently divides his time between his homes in Dallas, Texas, and Fort Lauderdale, Florida.